The
TRACTION ENGINE IN SCOTLAND
Alexander Hayward

First published in 2011 by
NMS Enterprises Limited – Publishing
a division of NMS Enterprises Limited
National Museums Scotland
Chambers Street, Edinburgh EH1 1JF

www.nms.ac.uk

All websites referred to in this publication were checked
before going to press.

British Library Cataloguing in
Publication Data
A catalogue record for this book
is available from the British Library.

ISBN: 978 1 905267 37 8 (hbk)
ISBN: 978 1 905267 58 3 (pbk)

Cover design: Mark Blackadder
Cover and title page image: 'Lancashire boiler en route
     to Alloa' (see page 82) (John R. Hume Collection)
Publication format:
     NMS Enterprises Limited – Publishing
Printed and bound in the United Kingdom
     by Bell & Bain Limited, Glasgow

Published by National Museums Scotland as one
of a number of titles based on museum scholarship
and partnership.

For a full listing of NMS Enterprises Limited – Publishing
titles and related merchandise:

www.nms.ac.uk/shop

CONTENTS

ACKNOWLEDGEMENTS

Alexander Hayward
National Museums Scotland

SHORTLY after I arrived in National Museums Scotland in 2005 to take up my post as Keeper of Science and Technology, I was taken to see the collections for which I was now responsible. Among these was a 1907 Marshall traction engine, its restoration well advanced. The opportunity was taken to complete this work in time for its centenary, and while this was underway the idea of creating a short publication to record the engine's history was born. Thanks to the support of Jane Carmichael, Director of Collections, and Lesley Taylor, Director of Publishing, that publication was able to grow into this book, allowing the Marshall to be presented in a much broader historical and technical context.

Many people have helped me with researching and writing this account. In the Museum I have received much encouragement and practical support from colleagues in the Department of Science and Technology: Alison Taubman, Alan Mills, Maureen Kerr, Alison Morrison-Low, Alastair Dodds and Klaus Staubermann. From the Department of Scotland and Europe, Dorothy Kidd and Kate MacKay have provided access to the Scottish Life Archive, and Elaine Edwards and Duncan Dornan in the National Museum of Rural Life have shared agricul-

tural expertise and access to the collections there. Mark Glancy, Andy McDougall and Morven Donald in the Museum's fine library have risen to the challenge of providing me with all manner of publications, and Nick Basden in Visitor Services alerted me to the interesting account of the life of the steam roller driver cited in chapter 3. Chris Cockburn in the Department of Conservation and Analytical Research provided information about the restoration of the Marshall, and Neil McLean and his colleagues in photography captured some great images. Maggie Wilson in the Image Licensing department did a wonderful job assisting in the picture research.

Outside the Museum I have also received much support. In Arbroath, Kirsten Couper kindly provided access to the Alexander Shanks material at the Signal Tower Museum; and through the good offices of Joanne Howdle photographs were generously contributed by Caithness Horizons Collections Trust in Thurso. Grateful thanks are also extended to Mike Ward and Peter Donaldson of Grampian Transport Museum in Alford, Aberdeenshire, for the use of historic photographs from their collections. Jim Murray, Librarian at the Royal Highland and Agricultural Society of Scotland, made me welcome in the Society's extensive library at Ingliston. Many people shared their knowledge: Tony Brown about the road steamers of R. W. Thomson and his contemporaries; Heather Holmes about Scottish agricultural engineers and implement makers; Elspeth King of Stirling Museum, Jane Petrie of Stirling Archives, and Elma Lindsay, Stirling Local History Officer, provided information about Raines, the local steam threshing contractors; and Geoff Hayes, Trevor Rees and Jim Wood from the Scottish Traction Engine Society shared information about Raines, Jock Mackay (from whom National Museums Scotland acquired the Marshall traction engine) and the early days of preservation. Bill Wells, the Road Locomotive Society's Records Officer, helped greatly with the identification of some of the engines pictured in historic photographs. Sir James Morrison-Low BT. kindly contributed his photograph album, providing a wonderful insight into steam preservation in the 1960s. The manuscript was read by Jim Wood, John Hume, Shirley Nicholson and Rosy Hayward, and benefited from their comments and suggestions. John Hume also contributed examples of the last days of working steam in Springburn and Slamannan, some photographs from his extensive collections, and generously provided the Foreword. My grateful thanks are extended to them all, and to those I may have omitted inadvertently.

Edinburgh, *April 2011*

PREFACE

Jane Carmichael
Director of Collections, National Museums Scotland

THE origins of today's National Museums Scotland lie in part in the Industrial Museum of Scotland founded in 1854. Its first Director was George Wilson, Professor of Technology at the University of Edinburgh, who was appointed in 1858. His vision, quoted from the Director's *Annual Report* of 1857, was, 'An industrial museum cannot be complete without illustrations of the existing state of the useful arts [i.e. technology] among the nations of the world'.

Although Wilson died before the Industrial Museum opened in 1862, he created a strand of enduring importance in its approach to collecting. Today the technology collections cover developments in aviation, engineering, transport, communications, and of course the subject of this book, steam power. They include a Boulton and Watt engine of 1786, one of the oldest surviving beam engines in the world and still in working order, and one of the last supersonic Concorde aircraft, G-BOAA, retired by British Airways in 2003. These collections are regarded as among the finest in the world.

The idea for this book began with a restoration project to bring the Museum's own Marshall traction engine back to working life for its centenary. From that project grew the more ambitious plan to use the Museum's wonderful example as the basis for a full history of the use of the steam traction engine in Scotland. It became clear that there was a superb range of archival material extant to include as illustration. In addition, with the restoration complete, the occasional steamings of the Museum's scarlet-liveried traction engine attracted considerable attention and excitement.

Transport and machinery driven by steam power now belong to a bygone age; its heyday lasted roughly a hundred years from the mid-nineteenth to the mid-twentieth century. The surviving examples seem possibly more picturesque than effective to modern eyes used to the miniaturisation of computing power. In this book, however, Alexander Hayward, the present Keeper of Science and Technology at National Museums Scotland, reminds us of how powerful and innovative these machines were and of their enormous impact on society and industry in their day. It is very much in the spirit of George Wilson's founding vision for the Museum.

Edinburgh, *April 2011*

FOREWORD

Professor John R. Hume OBE
Chairman, Royal Commission on the Ancient and Historical Monuments of Scotland

IT is a great pleasure to write a foreword for this pioneering study of steam traction engines and steam rollers in Scotland. The making of these machines on a large scale was a significant gap in the spectrum of Scottish engineering manufacture, though the innovative work of R.W. Thomson in developing rubber-tyred road steamers has long been recognised as highly significant. Other Scots engineers were also developing what could be called 'road locomotives' in the 1860s and 70s, but with nothing like the success of Fowler of Leeds, Marshall of Gainsborough, Burrell of Thetford, Aveling & Porter of Rochester, and Wallis & Steevens of Basingstoke. It was these English firms that created a model for the steam traction engine which persisted for more than half a century. Many English-built engines were used in Scotland, for heavy haulage, for agricultural purposes (especially threshing) and for road making and repair. Agricultural engines were displayed at the Royal Highland and other agricultural shows. In the 1920s development of internal-combustion engined analogues, more economical in both fuel and labour, ousted these fine machines for new construction, and then in the 1940s and 1950s for general use. The care and driving of these machines was a distinctive way of life: man and machine in a symbiotic relationship.

This volume discusses in a comprehensive way the rise, progress and decline of these characterful machines. By the time their use was falling into terminal decline people interested in engineering heritage, initially in England, were beginning to realise that the preservation of such engines was practical for individuals. Initially it was traction engines which proved most attractive, but when the supply of these dried up steam rollers proved a satisfactory alternative. Alexander Hayward discusses this phenomenon, which spread to Scotland in about 1960. Traction engine rallies and 'steam days' are still a part of summer life. Individual engines are in the collections of Summerlee Heritage, National Museums Scotland and Glasgow Museums, and there are many engines in private hands, notably in Aberdeenshire, with the members of the Deeside Steam and Vintage Club. The author's account of piecing together the history of National Museums Scotland's Marshall makes fascinating reading.

The author is to be congratulated on his success in drawing together a mass of material from a wide range of sources, to form a well-structured and accessible whole. Old 'steam buffs' like me will find this a delight, and I believe that it will intrigue and inform a much wider readership. There is something immensely likeable, and even lovable about these machines. They were, on good authority, designed and made with an eye to beauty of form, and often (as in the case of the National Museums Scotland's engine) painted to a very high standard. Their owners were generally very proud of them, for they were, even more than railway locomotives, in the public eye, conspicuous exemplars of the power and appeal of steam machinery. It is right that they should be celebrated in this way.

Glasgow, *April 2011*

FOWLER SINGLE-CYLINDER PLOUGHING ENGINE

Side view of a ploughing engine owned by Andrew Gilchrist, Carvenom, Fife, and photographed in c.1910. The cable winding drum is mounted horizontally beneath the boiler, between and behind the two men standing by the front and rear wheels. The large box between the front wheels provided storage for tools and parts for maintaining and repairing the engine and implements.

(© National Museums Scotland, SLA W504410)

Introduction

RAISING STEAM

RAISING STEAM

Setting the Historical and Technical Context

ONE of the larger and more colourful objects in the Science and Technology collections of National Museums Scotland is a Marshall general purpose traction engine. Dating from 1907, its restoration to full working order was completed in its centenary year in 2007. The Marshall worked for forty years in central Scotland, first for a timber merchant and then powering a travelling threshing machine operated by an agricultural contractor. It thus represents the application of steam power to both road transport and rural industry. This began in Scotland in the middle decades of the nineteenth century with the efforts of experimentally-minded engineers and progressive landowners, and ended around a hundred years later by which time petrol and diesel-engined machinery was becoming prevalent.

The Marshall, and the completion of its restoration by National Museums Scotland, has provided the impetus for this publication. The book is aimed at those with a broad interest in Scotland's industrial, rural and transport history and is intended to provide an overview of the use of steam power on Scottish roads and fields, allowing the museum's traction engine to be appreciated within its historical and technological context. In this regard, it is important to note that there were many versions and applications of the traction engine. Here the term is considered widely to include the simple traction engine (sometimes known as a general purpose traction engine, or agricultural locomotive), its predecessor the portable steam engine, and subsequent derivatives: the ploughing engine, road locomotive, road roller and the steam wagon[1] (but not the steam car).

Previous histories have presented the traction engine in Scotland as a part-player in larger thematic narratives, rather than the focus of a study in its own right. There are good reasons for this. As a power source in agriculture and road transport, the traction engine was outnumbered by the horse, and later by the farm tractor and motor lorry. As an engineering product it was eclipsed by the ships and locomotives for which Scotland became world famous.[2] Nonetheless, the subject merits further exploration. Hundreds of traction engines of all types were made in Scotland, and thousands of engines were at work here by the early twentieth century.[3] It is these histories, of production and use, which this book sets out to tell.

The study begins by examining steam road vehicles designed and made in Scotland, including the distinctive pattern of traction engine developed by Scottish makers between the 1850s and 1870s. Many of these, like Thomson's road steamer, were exported world-wide. By the later nineteenth century, English-made traction engines (such as the museum's Marshall) predominated in Scotland – in number and in their basic design – and these remained the standard until this technology became obsolete. One of the most successful of British steam-powered lorries, the Sentinel, was developed in Scotland, although manufacture was transferred to Shropshire during the First World War. All of these machines needed to attract buyers and users, so steam power was promoted through demonstrations and displays at field trials and trade shows. Engines were prepared to look especially attractive at such events, and research undertaken in connection with the restoration of the museum's Marshall suggests that it too may have been one of these. Even away from the showground, manufacturers were keen to promote their wares, and some English makers tried to attract Scottish buyers by specially branding their products.

The central part of the book is given over to a richly illustrated review of the uses of the traction engine in Scotland. Cultivation by steam was a niche use, where capital was available and the geography amenable. But for driving the mobile threshing machine, moving very heavy loads or constructing roads, steam was the most practical power until replaced by the internal combustion engine.

Thus traction engines were found throughout the mainland (chiefly the fertile and populous lowlands) and several of the Scottish isles. Steam was essentially a nineteenth-century phenomenon, but new portable engines little changed from the 1840s were still being supplied for use in Scottish sawmills operated by the Timber Corps during the Second World War.[4] Even as Scotland entered the Atomic Age at Dounreay in the 1950s, and for some time after, the solid longevity of the steam engine resulted in some local authorities keeping their fleets of road rollers at work.

Although such instances may simply appear to provide examples of technological conservatism, they also demonstrate tacit recognition by those in authority that steam represented an appropriate technology, simple and robust, with existing skills and infrastructure available for its operation and maintenance. In these situations, a prudent approach to business finances also ensured that equipment still in good condition continued to be used, rather than replaced just because it looked old fashioned.

By this time a nostalgic affection for traction engines was well developed in Scotland. From the 1950s a number of farmers and engineers purchased and restored engines for their own pleasure, and soon, in an echo of their appearance on showgrounds when new, these were

to be seen taking pride of place at vintage rallies and country fairs.

Museums too preserved examples of these machines, and the book concludes with a detailed examination of the life history of the Marshall engine in the National Museums Scotland, including its recent restoration to original working condition. This proved to be a very complex task, but the dividend has been a museum exhibit which not only shows what the century-old machine looked like when new, but also provides the smells, sounds and physical experience associated with its operation. This project has therefore been about more than simply physical preservation. To put the engine to work again, and then keep it fit and maintained for many more years of operation and public enjoyment, has meant that traditional engineering skills have had to be learned again. Preserving both the tangible and intangible in this way ensures that the museum can provide a range of insights into this striking manifestation of steam power.

A range of sources has been consulted in the preparation of this book. In addition to more recent works, a variety of historical sources have been used where available. These include makers' records and catalogues, advertisements, newspapers, journals, text books and technical reports. A key resource has been the Scottish Life Archive held by National Museums Scotland, which has for over half a century collected pictorial and documentary evidence of the nation's social and industrial history.[5] Constraints of space have meant that it has not been possible to include all the information that has

been unearthed, and thus the book provides more of an introduction to the subject rather than an encyclopaedic survey. In the course of this work a number of topics have been identified for further research, including more accurately quantifying the numbers and distribution of engines in Scotland, whether in agriculture, commercial transport or road construction. This would contribute to a better understanding of the impact of these machines on work practices and productivity, and on their associated communities. Much needs to be done on the design and manufacture of traction engines in Scotland, including identifying and studying the remains of surviving examples. The operations of the steam ploughing companies in the nineteenth century, or of later agricultural contractors, also merit deeper investigation. In many of these areas it has become clear however that there are very real challenges for the historian concerning the consistency, completeness, and dispersed location of the relevant information.

Nonetheless it is hoped that this book will lead to a broader appreciation of the overall place of the traction engine in Scottish life and industry.

Opposite page:

THRESHING IN ABERDEENSHIRE, *c.*1910

The demands of threshing time brought rural communities to work together. Here an unusually large group pose at Cruden Bay, Aberdeenshire, in front of a single-cylinder traction engine and threshing machine, both made by Ransomes, Sims & Jefferies of Ipswich. After they have dealt with the four corn stacks, they could look forward to a good meal, whisky and fiddle music, singing and dancing.

(© National Museums Scotland, SLA C2589)

ILLUSTRATED GLOSSARY

The Principal Types of Traction Engine used in Scotland

Portable Engine

An often-overlooked relative of the traction engine (and with which it is sometimes confused) is the portable engine. These had a combined boiler and engine, mounted on wheels but not self-moving, and so needing to be hauled to their workplace – note the horse shafts attached to the front of the engine. Power, typically for a threshing mill or saw bench, was taken by a long flat belt from the large flywheel (behind the chimney). Portable engines were quite simple to operate, as demonstrated by the young driver here.

MARSHALL PORTABLE ENGINE AT KIRKNEWTON, MIDLOTHIAN, c.1880

(© National Museums Scotland, SLA C13362)

Traction Engine

The traction engine was a self-moving combination of boiler and engine, used for hauling loads and providing power for stationary machinery. Rugged traction engines made specifically for hauling heavy loads were called road locomotives. This single-cylinder traction engine was made by Foden of Sandbach, Cheshire, *c.*1900, and owned by Davidsons of Dalkeith when this photograph was taken. The driver was Mr Combe and his engine looks shiny and well kept.

FODEN TRACTION ENGINE
AT MUIRPARK,
EAST LOTHIAN, *c.*1920

(© National Museums Scotland, SLA C2083)

ILLUSTRATED GLOSSARY

Ploughing Engine

The ploughing engine was a specialised traction engine which had a winch mechanism for hauling cultivating implements through the soil. Ploughing engines usually worked in pairs, one on each side of the field, pulling the implement to and fro. These 10-horsepower single-cylinder engines were made by Fowler of Leeds, *c*.1870, and had already had a long working life when bought by the Tweedie family of Coates in 1919.

FOWLER PLOUGHING ENGINES AT LONGNIDDRY, EAST LOTHIAN, *c*.1920

(© National Museums Scotland) SLA C12935)

Steam Roller

The steam roller had smooth wheels for compacting and shaping the road surface. This roller had a nominal weight of ten tons, and a two-cylinder compound engine. It was made by Aveling & Porter of Rochester, Kent, c.1920, and owned by William Dobson Limited, civil engineering contractors of Edinburgh.

AVELING & PORTER STEAM ROLLER AT PORT SETON, EAST LOTHIAN, c.1935

(© National Museums Scotland, SLA W532227A)

ILLUSTRATED GLOSSARY

Steam Wagon

The steam wagon had a compact steam engine and boiler mounted in a chassis which could carry a range of bodies for different loads – the precursor of the modern lorry.

There were two types of wagon: *overtype*, where the engine was carried on top of the boiler; and *undertype*, where the engine was carried beneath the chassis.

This overtype steam wagon was made by Richard Garrett of Leiston, Suffolk, *c*.1920, and owned by Anderson of Portsoy. The legal maximum speed of the wagon was eight miles per hour, and the licence disc is displayed on the side panel covering the two-cylinder compound engine.

GARRETT STEAM WAGON
AT PORTSOY HARBOUR,
c.1925
(© National Museums Scotland,
Scottish Life Archive)

References

1. This scope accords with that adopted by such bodies as the Road Locomotive Society, the principal historical organisation in this field, whose remit is the study of 'self propelled steam road engines and portable steam engines' (quote from *The Road Locomotive Society Journal*, vol. 63, no. 4, November 2010).

2. Published monographs providing historical context for the making and use of traction engines in Scotland include: J. L. Wood, *Scottish engineering: the machine makers* (2000); G. Oliver, *Motor trials and tribulations* (1993); T. McTaggart, *Pioneers of heavy haulage* (1985); Highland and Agricultural Society of Scotland, *Report on the present state of agriculture in Scotland* (1878); A. Fenton, *Scottish country life* (1999); G. Sprott, *The tractor in Scotland* (1978); G. Sprott, *Farming* (1995); regional studies such as I. Carter, *Farm life in northeast Scotland* (1979); and British studies such as W. Fletcher, *The history and development of steam locomotion on common roads* (1891); R. H. Clark, *The development of the English steam wagon* (1963); E. J. T. Collins, *Power availability and agricultural productivity in England and Wales 1840–1939* (1996); J. Brown, *Steam on the farm: a history of agricultural steam engines 1800 to 1950* (2008); and P. Dewey, *Iron harvests of the field: the making of farm machinery in Britain since 1800* (2008).

3. No single source of information regarding the numbers of traction engines used in Scotland has been located. For engines used in agriculture, Brown (2008), op. cit. (note 2), p. 36, cites the following outline statistics. In 1908 a census of agricultural steam engines in England and Wales recorded 13,630 units. A 1912 census for Great Britain recorded 16,959 engines, an increase of just over 3300. Some of this difference will have been made up by new engines put into use in England and Wales, but it seems reasonable to assume that a significant part of this increase is attributable to the inclusion of agricultural steam engines in Scotland. These would have comprised stationary steam engines in barns and mills, as well as portable, ploughing and traction engines, so the latter group may have totalled around 1000 units. To these need to be added road locomotives and steam wagons used in haulage, and steam rollers for road construction, making perhaps another 1000 or so. This suggests that the total number of traction engines, widely defined, in use in Scotland in the early twentieth century is unlikely to have been more than 2000–3000.

4. This approach to the history of technology, focussing on long histories of use rather than the instant of invention, is exemplified by D. Edgerton, *The shock of the old* (2006).

5. National Museums of Scotland, *The Scottish Life Archive [index and guide]* (1998).

Next page:

1907 MARSHALL TRACTION ENGINE

The Museum's engine at National Museum of Rural Life, Kittochside, in 2008.

(© National Museums Scotland)

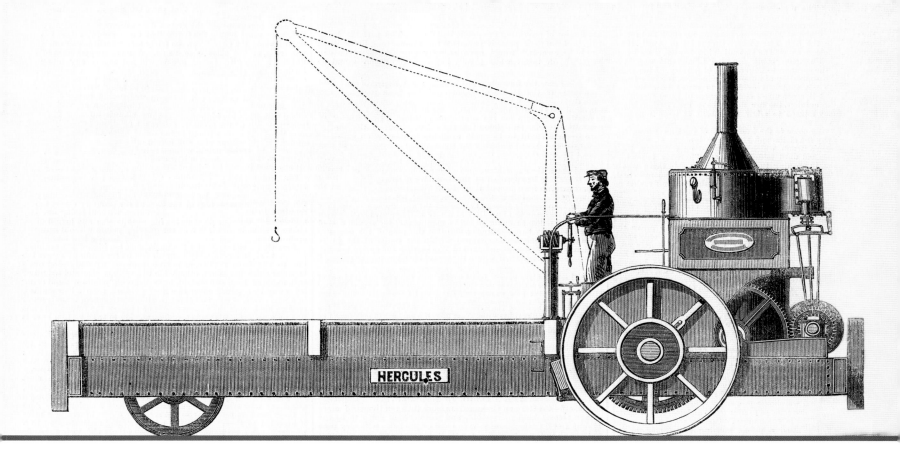

Chapter 1

MAKING STEAM

MAKING STEAM

Manufacturing Traction Engines in Scotland

FOR much of the nineteenth and twentieth centuries Scotland was renowned for its heavy engineering: steamships, locomotives, cranes, boilers, stationary engines and pumps, and the machine tools to make them, all exported across the globe.[1] This activity has understandably overshadowed the Scottish contribution to steam traction engine manufacture, but alongside the dominant English presence in this market there were also a number of Scottish makers.[2] For some of these engineers it is true that traction engine manufacture was just one part of their astonishingly diverse activity, but in Thomson's road steamer, and Alley & MacLellan's Sentinel steam lorry, we see examples of products which were more than just a sideline for their makers. These and their contemporary Scottish steam vehicles form the subject of this chapter. Collectively they illustrate broad themes of innovation and, through their export, the international reach of Scottish industry.

'Hunting shadows': precursors to the traction engine

James Watt had been alert to the possibility of a steam-powered vehicle since 1758 and he finally patented a design for a steam engine which could be used to drive a carriage in 1782. He had no intention of making such a carriage; the patent was instead intended to discourage others from exploring the idea.[3] Nonetheless, Ayrshire-born William Murdoch built a three-wheeled experimental model around 1784. Murdoch was then an engineer working for Watt in Cornwall, supervising the erection of beam engines for mine drainage. Neither Watt nor his partner Matthew Boulton wished to see Murdoch distracted from their business by developing his own invention and so they tried to dissuade Murdoch from pursuing it further.[4] In 1786 William Symington, son of a mechanic at the Wanlockhead lead mines in south west Scotland, also developed a model steam-powered carriage which was demonstrated in Edinburgh. Nothing further came of Symington's steam

carriage design, and he concentrated subsequently on developing the first successful steam boats.[5] In September that year Watt wrote to Boulton that

> *I am extremely sorry that W. M. [William Murdoch] still busys himself with the Stm. Carriage … in the meantime I wish W. could be brought to do as we do, to mind the business in hand, & let such as Symn. [Symington] … throw away their time and money hunting shadows.*[6]

Watt was right to be cautious, as making the transition from working model to a practical full-size vehicle was problematic. The first to achieve this in Britain was Richard Trevithick, Murdoch's Cornish contemporary and an advocate of the compact high pressure steam engine (in contrast to Watt's large low pressure engines). But even when Trevithick developed a number of full-size road and then railway locomotives in the early 1800s, commercial success eluded him.

Steam carriages in Scotland

In 1827 the 19-year-old James Nasmyth successfully demonstrated a model steam carriage to the Scottish Society of Arts in Edinburgh. This led to a full-size carriage being constructed at Anderson's foundry in Leith. In trials along the Queensferry Road it was able to carry eight passengers. According to Nasmyth, the Society 'did not attach any commercial value to my steam road carriage. It was merely as a matter of experiment that they had invited me to construct it.' Nasmyth dismantled the carriage and sold its components to pay for his engineering studies, later becoming renowned for his invention of the steam hammer.[7]

A number of other inventors and speculators were nevertheless convinced of the commercial potential of steam-powered coaches for passenger transport in cities and along trunk roads, building machines capable of travelling at 15 to 20 miles per hour. Acceptance of this novel technology was however hindered by occasional alarming boiler explosions or mechanical breakdowns. There was also deep-seated antagonism between the steam carriage proprietors and conservative authority figures, or those dependent on the established horse-based transport economy. They felt that steam carriages damaged the roads and were worried about loss of passengers.

Goldsworthy Gurney from London provided an example of the latest technology when two of his 'steam drags' were shipped to Scotland *circa* 1830. The boiler of one blew up whilst at Leith, but the other made some demonstration journeys around Glasgow in 1831.[8] Soon afterwards the scientist and engineer John Scott Russell designed a vehicle combining boiler, engine and passenger accommodation, for the Steam Carriage Company of Scotland. Six examples were built by Grove House Engine Works in Edinburgh. Russell's carriage incorporated an unusual rectangular boiler and great attention was given to the spring suspension, as he believed others' earlier designs had neglected this which had contributed to their mechanical unreliability. In April 1834 an hourly service was established between Glasgow and Paisley, but according to Russell's supporters the hostile local road trustees sought to sabotage the service by making the road impassable with a thick

covering of stone. After running through this for some months, one of the carriages broke a wheel. The carriage tilted over and its weight came to rest on the boiler, which exploded and killed five passengers. The Court of Session subsequently banned the carriages from running in Scotland, but two were sent to London where they were trialled during early 1835.[9] Russell ceased his steam carriage endeavours and went on to become an eminent naval architect, including collaborating with I. K. Brunel on the design of the huge steamship 'Great Eastern'.

From this time on, railways assumed increasing importance in providing inter-urban transport, against which steam carriages struggled to compete. Some inventors carried on making passenger vehicles, such as the steam carriage made by Thomas Rickett of Buckingham for the Earl of Caithness. This was driven from Inverness to Barrogill Castle near John o' Groats in 1860, introducing road steam to the Highlands.[10] In Scotland this approach to steam transport culminated in some idiosyncratic one-off vehicles like the lavish steam coach built for Charles Randolph (founder of the noted marine engineering firm Randolph Elder & Company) by Dübs of Glasgow in 1872,[11] the 'Craigievar Express', a small three-wheeler assembled by Aberdeenshire postman Andrew Lawson between 1895 and 1897,[12] and the steam cart built for use on the Salvesen family estate in Polmont in 1896.[13] The real significance of all these vehicles lies however in their anticipating the function of the personal motor car which was to proliferate during the early twentieth century.

Meanwhile others concentrated on developing larger vehicles intended for hauling heavier loads. Three inter-related considerations preoccupied designers in this work: providing sufficient tractive grip for the driving wheels; protecting the vehicle from shock and vibration caused by rough stone-paved roads; and in turn preventing damage to the road surface caused by the propelling action of the wheels and the weight of the vehicle.

Getting a grip:
Bray traction engines in Scotland

In 1856 the marine engineer William Bray from Kent patented a traction engine driving wheel with lugs (similar to the paddle wheels on a steamship) which could be made to project by varying amounts through the face of the wheel and so increase its grip on the road. One of Bray's traction engines, fitted with these patent driving wheels on a sprung axle, and with a crane attached, was used at the 1862 International Exhibition in London. By this time, the Scottish born and trained engineer Daniel Kinnear Clark had been hired by Bray's Traction-Engine Company as a consultant

designer, having worked previously for both the North British Railway and the Great North of Scotland Railway. Clark's final design of traction engine, incorporating Bray's patent, not surprisingly largely followed railway practice: the horizontal locomotive boiler was mounted on a frame to which were attached two cylinders in line with the rear axle.[14] Several of these were built between 1866 and 1876 by Dübs & Company at their Glasgow Locomotive Works.[15] At least one of Clark's road locomotives was built with plain straked iron wheels in place of Bray's patent wheel.

**'ABDUL AZIZ'
ROAD ENGINE, 1866**

This road engine was built in 1866 by Dübs & Company, Glasgow, for the Ottoman Company for use on routes to Damascus.

(© Glasgow City Council, Licensor www.scran.ac.uk)

Alexander Chaplin & Company, Glasgow

Alexander Chaplin & Company also produced Bray-wheeled traction engines. The firm was established in 1849 and a wide range of robust machinery went on to be produced at Chaplin's Cranstonhill Engine Works in Port Street, Glasgow. This notably included steam-powered cranes and excavators, pumps, stationary and marine steam engines, as well as railway locomotives for shunting.[16]

Chaplin favoured using vertical boilers rather than the locomotive type which was a little more complex to manufacture. The firm's early traction engine looked like a road-going version of their basic railway locomotives with a vertical boiler mounted in a riveted side frame and the wheels driven through gearing by a vertical steam engine.[17] In 1862 Chaplin constructed a similar machine but with a large load-carrying platform in front of the boiler, able to carry 15–20 tons. Named 'Hercules' it could be fitted with a crane. Indeed, Chaplin found it so useful in Glasgow that it could not be spared for the International Exhibition that year as had been intended.[18] Instead a steam crane was sent, and this involvement with the Exhibition may have provided an introduction to Clark's design of traction engine with Bray's driving wheel. Shortly afterwards, Chaplin made a traction engine along similar lines but with a vertical boiler in place of the locomotive type.[19] Two photographs of this machine, dated December 1863 and captioned '15 HP traction engine, Chaplin's and Bray's Patents, (Combined)' are in the collections of National Museums Scotland (see page 20).[20] The Bray patent referred to clearly relates to the driving wheel design, whilst the Chaplin patent relates to the boiler design. To improve the efficiency of the vertical boiler, Chaplin had introduced some water tubes which hung down into the firebox. These increased the heating surface and promoted water circulation for rapid steaming, and were arranged so that heat from the fire circulated around the water tubes rather than passing straight up the chimney. In May 1866 one of these engines was described as having two cylinders of 7-inch bore and 14-inch stroke, three speeds (2, 4 or 8 miles per hour) and weighing 12 tons empty. It had been

> ... severely tested in Glasgow by drawing marine boilers of the heaviest class (the weights being from 30 to 40 tons), from the works of Messrs. R. Napier and Sons, Messrs. Tod and Macgregor, and Messrs. Randolph Elder and Co., to vessels lying at the large crane, the engine and load having sometimes to pass en route over Glasgow bridge .... The engine has also conveyed a small iron vessel, weighing, with the truck upon which it was carried, about 45 tons, a distance of two miles over ordinary paved street, mounting in the course of its journey an incline of about 1 in 30. Such performances are entirely satisfactory.[21]

Two 12-horsepower traction engines were built by Chaplin in 1866 and 1867 for export to Fontaine & Smith in Mauritius, presumably for use in the sugar

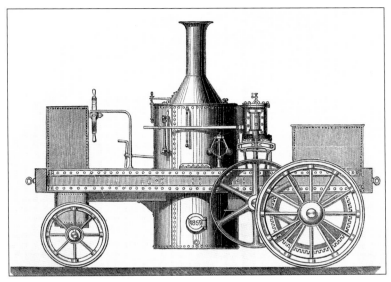

ALEXANDER CHAPLIN & COMPANY, GLASGOW

Left:

CHAPLIN'S TRACTION ENGINE, 1859

Chaplin's vertical boiler traction engine, from the *Catalogue of the 1862 Exhibition*, vol. 1, class VIII, p 14.

(© National Museums Scotland)

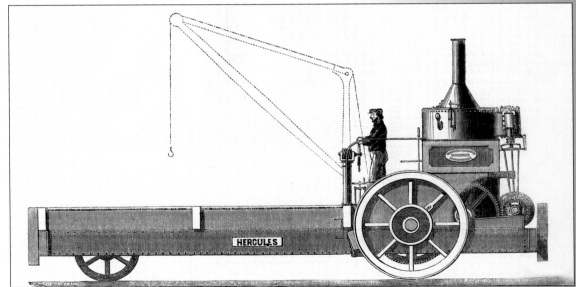

Right:

CHAPLIN'S STEAM TRACTION AND CARRYING WAGON, 'HERCULES', 1862

Engraving of Chaplin's 'Steam traction and carrying wagon' from *The Engineer*, 23 May 1862, p. 316.

(© National Museums Scotland)

ALEXANDER CHAPLIN & COMPANY, GLASGOW

Opposite page (above and below):

CHAPLIN STEAM ROLLER

'Improved Steam Roller / A. Chaplin & Co Glasgow', *c*.1878. McKendrick, Ball and Company, noted at the top left-hand corner of the photograph, were Chaplin's London agents.

(© Scottish Motor Museum, Licensor www.scran.ac.uk)

Above: [side-on view]

CHAPLIN'S 15-HORSEPOWER TRACTION

The projections through the rear wheel to increase grip (Bray's patent) can be seen, and there is a cloth sheet for covering the engine rolled up underneath the side-mounted water tanks.

Photographed in December 1863.

Below: [3/4 rear view]

The engine is photographed outside Chaplin's Cranstonhill Engine Works in December 1863. The cloth sheet covering the engine is now rolled down.

(© National Museums Scotland, T.1929.40.1–2)

ROBERT DOUGLAS STEAM ROLLER

The simple steam roller made by Robert Douglas of Kirkcaldy, *c*.1870. The stoker's head can been seen behind the steersman's feet. The large rectangular tank held water for the boiler.

(© National Museums Scotland)

plantations. A 15-horsepower traction engine was supplied to Chaplin (perhaps to be used for heavy haulage by the firm) in 1867; and a much smaller traction engine of 6-horsepower was made in 1871 – this was for Jonas Shobrooke's farm in North Lew, Devon.[22]

Chaplin also made two road rollers, both weighing 15 tons. They had a vertical boiler and engine similar to that used in Chaplin's steam cranes, with gear drive to the two front rollers and steering from the rear. The first was built in August 1877 for the Board of Police of Glasgow. It would appear that this was a success, and that the authorities wished to support local manufacture, as another roller followed in September 1878 for the Magistrates and Council of Glasgow.[23] Chaplin's 1879 catalogue also mentions rollers of 10 and 20 tons weight,[24] but there are no surviving records to indicate that any of these were built. By this time Aveling & Porter in Kent had developed their very successful and long-lived steam roller design, making it difficult for others to enter this market. Chaplin's engine registers indicate the firm had by now constructed around 2000 other machines, so even allowing for a handful of pre-Bray pattern traction engines, constructed in the late 1850s, it is clear that traction engines and road rollers were only a minor part of the company's business.

Robert Douglas, Kirkcaldy

Around 1870 Robert Douglas of Kirkcaldy also built a small steam roller. It had a vertical boiler and a single-cylinder horizontal steam engine, and was steered from

the front with an attractive cast-iron ship's wheel. It is likely that this was an experimental machine, or was produced in response to a specific local need, as Douglas went on to concentrate on much larger machinery through his partnership in the millwrighting and engineering firm of Douglas & Grant.

R. W. Thomson and the road steamer

More success was found by R.W. Thomson and his road steamers developed during the 1860s and 1870s. These were strongly made and powerful machines, capable of hauling heavy loads at a good speed. Significantly they were produced in quantity and some had long working lives.

Thomson was born in Stonehaven, Aberdeenshire, in 1822. He was a prolific inventor and engineer, and is probably best known for being the first to patent a pneumatic tyre in 1845. This was tried on some horse-drawn vehicles but proved too expensive for widespread adoption, so his idea lapsed until later rediscovered by John Dunlop. After working in North Borneo, where he saw the value of a traction engine able to haul coal from mines to the coast, Thomson returned to Scotland in 1862. He set up as a consulting engineer in Edinburgh and turned his attention to improving the performance of traction engines, recognising the importance of tyre design in this. In 1867 Thomson patented his 'Improved Elastic Tyres' made of vulcanised rubber. The patent specified three types of tyre surface: smooth, thick, rubber bands stretched around the wheel circumference; a

means of protecting the smooth bands with metal plates attached around the periphery; and a tyre with corrugations across its face for increased grip. The 'Improved Elastic Tyres' had

> … *a bearing surface of greater extent circumferentially than ordinary rigid and unyielding tyres, in consequence of which they do not grind the surface of the roadway nor sink into it, and they thus enable the steam carriage to be propelled over bad roads with less power than that required with rigid tyres. They also admit of the ordinary springs being dispensed with, and consequently of the driving power being applied to the wheels by means of simpler gearing or mechanism than has hitherto been found requisite.*[25]

Alluding to Bray's wheel design, or the simple iron-plated wheels typical of other English traction engines, *Chambers's Encyclopaedia* of 1868 notes (in an entry probably written by Thomson himself) that

> … *the wheels hitherto in use required projections of some kind on the face of the tires to give the requisite bite. Those projections necessarily destroy the roads. Mr Thomson's wheels do not injure the roads in the slightest degree … nor is the machinery injured by jolting. The carriage rolls along as easily as if it were afloat.*[26]

Thomson's design of traction engine with his rubber-tyred wheels came to be known as road steamers. They had a vertical boiler mounted at the rear of a strong riveted frame. The double-cylinder horizontal engine was mounted on top of the frame, driving the two rear wheels through a train of gears providing two speeds. The stoker stood on a platform at the rear, and the driver, with steering wheel and engine controls, sat above the single front wheel. Like Chaplin before him, Thomson was determined to improve the efficiency of the vertical boiler. He developed his own design which had a spherical copper pot nearly filling the firebox space above the fire, patenting this in 1865.[27]

Thomson started making road steamers around 1868 in his own small workshop in Leith, the centre of engineering manufacturing near Edinburgh. One of the first road steamers was exported to Labuan in Borneo for coal haulage. Another went to rural Queensland where it was unable to cope with rough unmade roads and was sold on, ultimately ending up in Western Australia where it was used for haulage around Perth and Freemantle.[28] Thomson's ill health, and a desire to see his road steamer idea deliver him some financial return, led him to transfer their manufacture to nearby T. M. Tennant & Company in 1869, and explore licensing their manufacture to other large firms.[29]

T. M. Tennant & Company, Leith

Tennant operated the Bowershall Iron & Engine Works in Leith, a larger manufactory than Thomson's works, and better equipped to cope with the demand for road steamers. Tennants were prolific engineers and even in 1862 their product range included stationary steam engines, water wheels and turbines, locomotives and 'traction or roadway engines' of 10, 12, 15 and 20 horsepower. Portable engines with locomotive boilers, and one or two cylinders, were also made. Commencing in 1870 around 40–50 road steamers of between 6- to 12-horsepower are believed to have been made, before Tennant & Company vacated their works around 1873. To these can be added the dozen or so that Thomson constructed previously in his own works.[30]

The advance of the road steamers

The road steamers evidently made an impressive sight, and were reported widely around the world in the technical press and newspapers including the *Scotsman*, *Illustrated London News*, *Scientific American*, and *Brisbane Courier*. Many of the steamers were given names such as 'Enterprise', 'Pioneer', 'Advance' and 'Progress', reflecting the hopes vested in this promising technology. Some were tested around Leith and Edinburgh, hauling both passengers in carriages and trains of heavily-laden wagons. The Earl of Dunmore, a keen exponent of steam-powered cultivation, tested a Thomson 8-horsepower engine (with specially widened rear wheels) hauling a medium plough in the summer of 1870. John Head, from Ransomes, Sims & Head of Ipswich, Suffolk, then brought a large plough (destined for Russia where it would be pulled by 18 bullocks) to Dunmore to see how the steamer would handle it.

When he [Head] saw the engine move the great plough through the land he said he could not have believed it could have accomplished the work. Mr Head then went to Edinburgh, and took a license from Mr Thomson to make engines. … Ever since that trial, which was quite private, they had been almost pestered with draughtsmen from some of the large towns in England coming and copying the engine … .[31]

Among the road steamers constructed by Ransomes, Sims & Head were four large engines for hauling passengers and mail in the new 'Government Steam Train' between Jhelum and Rawalpindi. This project was championed by Lieutenant R. E. Crompton, a trained engineer who was an enthusiastic advocate of mechanical transport. Before commencing the service in India, Crompton conducted a thorough trial with one of the road steamers in the autumn of 1871, travelling between Ipswich and Edinburgh. The return journey covered 850 miles and at times speeds reached 25 miles per hour.[32] Other English firms which took out a manufacturing licence with Thomson included Charles Burrell of Thetford, Norfolk, who made seven road steamers in 1871. Three of these were exported to Turkey and one to Brazil.[33] Robey of Lincoln also built 33 Thomson road steamers between 1870 and 1877, sending some as far afield as Auckland, Moscow and Valparaiso.[34] Licence-building of Thomson's design even extended to the United States, where from 1871 D. D. Williamson arranged for twelve road steamers to

be manufactured by the Locomotive Works of Paterson (New Jersey). Williamson varied the boiler design and marketed the engines as the 'Williamson Road Steamer and Steam Plow', and they were used across North America.[35]

Around the world, Thomson's road steamers and their derivatives played an important role in popularising the idea of the mechanisation of road transport and cultivation, although they were not universally successful. Some were scrapped after only a few years, or in at least one instance converted into a stationary steam engine. One issue was the capacity and hard-wearing of the rubber tyres, which were of variable quality. A few users had trouble with the 'pot' boiler and replaced it with a different design for better steam generation. Other machines however achieved remarkable service. These include the fleet of road steamers used for heavy haulage around the River Clyde until the 1930s, which are discussed in chapter 3.

Other traction engineers in Leith

Coinciding with, and without doubt stimulated by Thomson's road steamers, there was a flurry of engine-building by others in Leith. In 1869 Todd built a two-person steam carriage with small vertical boiler and engine. A steam bus followed in 1872, in which year Todd also made a fast locomotive-boilered road engine for use abroad.[36] From 1865 the Locomotives Act (better known as the 'Red Flag Act') placed severe restrictions on the speed and use of traction engines on British

Thomson's road steamers

Above: 'THE DERWENT', THOMSON ROAD STEAMER

Thomson-built road steamer 'The Derwent' photographed when new.

(© Science Museum/SSPL)

Above (right): THOMSON'S ROAD STEAMER

A road steamer hauling a specimen tree in a special carriage.

(© Museum of English Rural Life, University of Reading)

Right: 'ENTERPRISE', ROAD STEAMER

Road steamer 'Enterprise' with a heavy load of four wagons in Labuan.

(© Museum of English Rural Life, University of Reading)

roads,[37] so export markets provided the only opportunity for designing and constructing machines capable of travelling legally at over four miles per hour. In 1870 Andrew Nairn launched his steam omnibus for service in Edinburgh, and later that year designed his own road steamer, again with a vertical boiler, and a vertical engine placed directly behind it. This was intended for hauling ploughs and loads on soft ground, and used tarred rope tightly coiled around the wheel in place of Thomson's rubber tyre. Metal shoes were fixed around the face of the wheels to protect the rope. In 1872 a road locomotive designed by Nairn was constructed by J. & T. Dale of Kirkcaldy for export to New Zealand.[38]

ROAD STEAMER WITH VERTICAL BOILER AND REAR MOUNTED VERTICAL ENGINE (rear and side view)

This machine is very similar to Nairn's design illustrated in *The Engineer*, 14 October 1870, p. 259.

(© Museum of English Rural Life, University of Reading)

The influence of Thomas Aveling

It is noticeable that Chaplin, Thomson, and their contemporaries from Scotland, were almost wholly devoted to using a vertical boiler and a separate engine mounted together on a frame in their designs, to the extent that this might be described as defining a Scottish pattern of traction engine. This was in contrast to the English makers who, by the 1870s, had largely adopted Thomas Aveling's layout for the traction engine, in which the proven and efficient horizontal locomotive pattern boiler provided an integral frame, or chassis, to which the engine and cast- or wrought-iron wheels were attached directly.

Aveling's prototype traction engine was created in 1858 at his engineering works in Rochester, Kent, by taking a Clayton & Shuttleworth horse-drawn portable engine of typical design (locomotive boiler with the engine mounted upon it) and rendering it self-moving by adding a chain drive from the engine to one of the rear wheels. Aveling's first engine still needed to be steered by horse, but in 1860 a steering mechanism was added for a front-mounted steersman. From 1862 a steam jacket was added around the cylinder to improve the efficiency of the engine, and in 1870 a most important improvement was introduced. This was Aveling's patented feature of extending the outer sideplates of the firebox to create 'hornplates' for supporting the crankshaft and transmission, and making possible the substitution of a train of strong gears in place of the chain drive. By this date the steering position had moved to the footplate (alongside the driver behind the boiler), and this whole package set the pattern for nearly all traction engines in the later nineteenth and early twentieth centuries.[39] Even the English makers of road steamers ultimately embraced Aveling's design.

One early Scottish engineer connected with Aveling was John Gray, proprietor of Uddingston Iron Works in Lanarkshire. In 1862 he supplied two ploughing engines to New Zealand. These both resembled Aveling's chain-drive traction engines of the time, and were most likely made in Rochester. Even though the engines carried the wording 'John Gray & Co.', his contribution was probably restricted to designing and adding the windlass gear for hauling the plough.[40]

By 1880 the popularity of the road steamer design had waned. With Thomson's early death in 1873, and the growing domination of the more numerous English makers, particularly Aveling, subsequent Scottish makers also adopted the orthodox English pattern of traction engine. None however achieved the impact of Thomson's design, or were constructed in anywhere near the same numbers.

Alexander Shanks & Sons, Arbroath

The company of Alexander Shanks & Sons operated the Dens Iron Works in Arbroath from 1840, and the firm's catalogues of the 1870s include a wide range of cranes and pumps, and stationary, portable and marine engines and boilers. In 1876 a 'Patent Road Locomotive Engine' was offered in six sizes from 4–14 horsepower, weighing

ALEXANDER SHANKS & SONS

Above and right:

PATENT ROAD LOCOMOTIVE

From the *Illustrated and descriptive catalogue of the manufactures of Alexander Shanks & Sons, Engineers* (*c.*1876), pp. 58 and 59.

(© Angus Council, Cultural Services/ Signal Tower Museum, Arbroath)

PATENT ROAD LOCOMOTIVE ENGINE.

THIS illustration represents a ROAD LOCOMOTIVE ENGINE with single cylinder, which is placed on the forward part of the boiler, and is surrounded by a jacket in direct communication with it ; the steam is taken into the cylinder from a dome connected with the jacket.　Priming is by this means prevented, the use of steam-pipes either inside or outside the boiler is rendered needless, and a considerable economy in fuel is effected.　The crank-shaft brackets are formed out of the side-plates of the fire-box extended upwards and backwards in one piece.　This arrangement produces a combination of much strength and lightness.　The driving-wheels are of wrought iron, and are fitted with compensating motion for turning sharp curves without disconnecting either wheel ; they carry about 85 per cent. of the weight of the Engine.　The Engine is steered from the foot-plate.　The boiler is made of best best quality plates, and tested with cold water to 260 lbs. on the square inch ; the fire-box is of Lowmoor iron.

Each Engine is supplied with steam-pressure gauge and extra safety valve, a complete set of wrenches, screw-hammer, firing tools, oil can, spare gauge glasses, and driving-wheel studs or paddles, free of extra charge.

The working expenses, including wear and tear with interest on capital, vary from 1¼d. per ton per mile for continuous work under favourable conditions of road and load, to 3d. per ton per mile for short distances with return journey unloaded.

The subjoined Table gives the power, speed, weight, and other general particulars of the most ordinary sizes of these Road Locomotives :—

Nominal Horse Power.	Consumption of Fuel per Diem.	Speed in Miles per Hour.		Load in Tons drawn on good Roads.		Weight on Road in Tons.	Ship's Measurement in Tons.
		Slow.	Fast.	Up 1 in 12.	On a Level.		
4	5 Cwt.	1 to 2½	3 to 4	8	10 to 15	7	12
6	6 „	„	„	10	15 „ 20	9	16
8	8 „	„	„	15	20 „ 25	11	20
10	10 „	„	„	20	25 „ 30	13	24
12	12 „	„	„	25	30 „ 40	15	28
14	14 „	„	„	30	40 „ 50	17	32

NOTE.—The above is the *nominal power* only ; the *actual* power given out is much greater.

LONDON OFFICE, 27 LEADENHALL STREET, E.C.

Above:

AVELING & PORTER ROAD LOCOMOTIVE

The similarity to the engine catalogued by Shanks is very apparent.

(© Museum of English Rural Life, University of Reading)

Right:

IMPROVED PORTABLE STEAM ENGINE

'Improved Portable Steam Engine' from the *Illustrated and descriptive catalogue of the manufactures of Alexander Shanks & Sons, Engineers* (*c.*1876), p 57.

(© Angus Council, Cultural Services/ Signal Tower Museum, Arbroath)

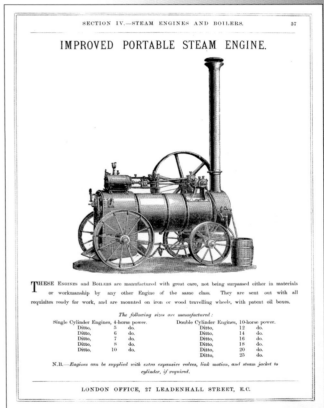

SECTION IV.—STEAM ENGINES AND BOILERS. 57

IMPROVED PORTABLE STEAM ENGINE.

THESE ENGINES and BOILERS are manufactured with great care, not being surpassed either in materials or workmanship by any other Engine of the same class. They are sent out with all requisites ready for work, and are mounted on iron or wood travelling wheels, with patent oil boxes.

The following sizes are manufactured :

Single Cylinder Engines, 4-horse power.		Double Cylinder Engines, 10-horse power.	
Ditto,	5 do.	Ditto,	12 do.
Ditto,	6 do.	Ditto,	14 do.
Ditto,	7 do.	Ditto,	16 do.
Ditto,	8 do.	Ditto,	18 do.
Ditto,	10 do.	Ditto,	20 do.
		Ditto,	25 do.

N.B.—*Engines can be supplied with extra expansive valves, link motion, and steam jacket to cylinder, if required.*

LONDON OFFICE, 27 LEADENHALL STREET, E.C.

from 7–17 tons, but by 1878 the smallest and largest sizes were dropped from the range. These engines show a distinct likeness to Aveling & Porter's market-leading road locomotive of the time, but it is unlikely Shanks would have simply copied Aveling's design and risked litigation for infringing his patent. Thus it may be that Shanks was offering rebranded Aveling engines. This practice was not unknown in the nineteenth century, and an order book for 1882 shows clearly that Shanks themselves supplied their own stationary steam engines marked with the final seller's name instead of their own. By the 1880s road locomotives were dropped from Shanks's catalogue, although locomotive-boilered portable engines were still offered in eleven sizes ranging from 6–30 horsepower. None of the catalogues give any indication of the number of road locomotives actually built or sold, or provide any testimonials from users, so the precise scale and nature of Shanks's traction engine endeavours remains ripe for further exploration.[41]

Bow McLachlan & Company, Paisley

Probably the last, and largest, traction engines made commercially in Scotland were those by Bow McLachlan & Company of Paisley. Their principal activity was shipbuilding, including marine engines[42], but at this time engineering companies prided themselves on their versatility and ability to satisfy a customer's order. In January 1897 they completed two 10-horsepower compound traction engines for the Manica Trading Company in Rhodesia (Zimbabwe). These were intended to replace horses and mules which were unable to cope with the extreme climate. Of basically orthodox design, the journal *Engineering* noted that:

The engines … have been specially designed for the country to be traversed. They are of exceptionally broad gauge, and the firebox stands so high that streams of 4 ft. in depth may be crossed without extinguishing the fires. The fuel to be used is wood, which will be stored at stations along the route, and the engines are provided with tanks sufficiently large to carry a 12 hours' supply of water.[43]

No further orders for similar engines appear to have been received by Bow McLachlan.

By the end of the nineteenth century it was clear that English makers had captured the market within Britain and its colonies for traction engines, road rollers and related vehicles. The combined production of the leading English makes such as Aveling & Porter, Burrell, and Fowler could be numbered in thousands, in contrast to a total Scottish output over the preceding five decades of probably one to two hundred machines at most. But in the specialised field of steam wagon manufacture, Scottish makers were still to make an impact.

Steam wagons

In 1896 the Locomotives on Highways Act was introduced, removing many of the restrictions imposed by the 'Red Flag' Act and subsequent legislation.[44] As a

Advertisements and Promotion

D. STEWART & CO. (1902) LTD.,
SOLE BUILDERS FOR SCOTLAND OF

Thornycroft Steam Waggons

Illustration of 5 ton waggon.   45 brake horse-power.

THORNYCROFT WAGGONS EMBODY THE RESULT OF 9 YEARS' PRACTICAL EXPERIENCE.

WRITE FOR PRICES AND PARTICULARS, STATING REQUIREMENTS.

AGENTS REQUIRED WHERE NOT REPRESENTED.

LONDON ROAD IRON WORKS,
GLASGOW.

Left:

STEWART-THORNYCROFT WAGON, 1905

Advertisement for Stewart-Thornycroft steam wagon. The vehicle illustrated appears to be a Chiswick-built Thornycroft carrying a London registration, indicating that the printing block was supplied by Thornycroft to Duncan Stewart's company for publicity use.

(© National Museums Scotland; source, *The Motor World*, 4 November 1905, p. 1091)

Below:

SENTINEL LORRIES READY FOR DELIVERY, 1907

Five new Sentinel lorries, painted and ready for delivery. The original caption for this image states that all were despatched on the same day, an indication that by the date this photograph was taken the two-year-old Sentinel wagon design was already being produced in some quantity.

(© National Museums Scotland; source, *The Motor World*, 27 April 1907, p. 443)

SCOTTISH TRACTION ENGINEERS

Summary List

The following list includes designers and makers of traction engines and related vehicles (excluding steam cars) in Scotland identified from sources referred to during the preparation of this book. More names may be identified as research into this field continues.

Alley & MacLellan Limited (Polmadie): made Sentinel steam wagons (1905–1915)

Anderson's foundry (Leith): made parts for James Nasmyth's steam carriage (1827)

Belhaven Engineering & Motors Limited (Wishaw): made steam wagons (1907–1915)

Bow McLachlan & Company (Paisley): made traction engines (1897)

Bridges (North Berwick): constructed steam engines and plough for the Marquis of Tweeddale (c.1860)

Alexander Chaplin & Company (Glasgow): made traction engines and road rollers (c.1859–1878)

J. & T. Dale (Kirkcaldy): made a road locomotive to Nairn's design (1872)

Robert Douglas (Kirkcaldy): made a steam roller (c.1870)

Dübs & Company (Glasgow): builder of Randolph's steam carriage and D. K. Clark's design of locomotive-style traction engines (1866–1876)

N. & D. Fraser & Sons Limited (Arbroath): made a steam wagon (c.1920)

Glasgow Motor Lorry Company Limited (Glasgow): made 'Halley' steam wagons (1901–1906)

John Gray & Company (Uddingston): converted and supplied ploughing engines of Aveling origin (1862)

Grove House Engine Works (Edinburgh): made steam carriages to John Scott Russell's design (1834)

Hawthorns & Company (Leith): made Nairn's steam bus (1870)

Robert Morton & Sons Limited (Wishaw) (from 1907 Belhaven Engineering and Motors Limited): made steam wagons to Liquid Fuel Engineering Company design (c.1905–1906)

Nairn (Leith): designer of steam bus, road steamer and road locomotive (1870–1872)

Alexander Shanks & Sons (Arbroath): catalogued portable engines and Aveling pattern road locomotives (c.1876–1880)

Slight (Edinburgh): made James Usher's steam cultivator (1851)

A. & W. Smith and Company (Glasgow): made a portable engine (c.1860)

D. Stewart & Company (1902) Limited (Glasgow): made Stewart-Thornycroft steam wagons c.1902–1907, thereafter Stewart steam wagons (c.1902–1914)

T. M. Tennant & Company (Leith): made portable engines, 'traction and roadway engines' and Thomson's design of road steamers (c.1862–1873)

R. W. Thomson (Leith): designed and made road steamers (c.1868–1869)

Leonard Todd (Leith): made a steam carriage, steam bus and road locomotive (1869–72)

John Yule (Glasgow): made a large steam wagon (1870)

References

1. J. L. Wood, *Scottish engineering: the machine makers* (2000).
2. For a historical overview of Scottish motor vehicle manufacture, including brief reference to steam vehicles, see G. Oliver, *Motor trials and tribulations* (1993).
3. B. Marsden, *Watt's perfect engine: steam and the age of invention* (2004), pp. 178–79.
4. W. Fletcher, *The history and development of steam locomotion on common roads* (1891), pp. 28–34.
5. Ibid., pp. 37–40.
6. James Watt, 12 September 1786, quoted in H. W. Dickinson and R. Jenkins, *James Watt and the steam engine* (1927, facsimile edition 1981), p. 61.
7. J. Nasmyth (ed.) and S. Smiles, *James Nasmyth Engineer: an autobiography* (1883), p. 120–22, quote from p. 122.
8. Fletcher (1891), op. cit. (note 4), pp. 97–102; www.steamcar.net/artgurn.html [accessed March 2011]. The description 'drag' was a reference to a type of horse carriage popular at this time.
9. Fletcher (1891), op. cit. (note 4), pp. 133–37; *Mechanics' Magazine*, vol. 22, no. 602 (21 February 1835), p. 370.
10. *The Engineer*, 19 October 1860, p. 254; 2 November 1860, p. 290.
11. W. Fletcher, *English and American steam carriages and traction engines* (1904, facsimile edition 1973), pp. 42–43.
12. Grampian Transport Museum, *The Craigievar Express* (1999).
13. www.motorbase.com/manufacturer/by-id/1486487805 [accessed March 2011]
14. W. J. Hughes, *A century of traction engines* (1972), pp. 45–54; M. R. Lane, *Pride of the road* (1976), p. 55.
15. Hughes (1972), op. cit. (note 14), pp. 55, 57; M. R. Lane (1976), op. cit. (note 14), pp. 55–56.
16. Notes and bibliography on Alexander Chaplin & Company in 'A–Z of Scottish engineering firms', Department of Science and Technology, National Museums Scotland.
17. Commissioners of the International Exhibition of 1862, *Illustrated catalogue of the industrial department*, British division, vol. 1, class VIII, p. 14.
18. *The Engineer*, 23 May 1862, p. 316.
19. D. K. Clark, *The exhibited machinery of 1862: a cyclopaedia of the machinery represented at the International Exhibition* (1864), p. 334.
20. National Museums Scotland [T.1929.401.1 and 2]; J. L. Wood, 'A Bray's patent engine by Alex Chaplin & Co., of Glasgow', in *The Road Locomotive Society Journal*, vol. 32, no. 2, June 1979, pp. 45–49.
21. *Engineering*, 4 May 1866, p. 295.
22. The engines were numbered respectively 662, 888, 346 and 1228 in 'Register of engines &c. manufactured and sold by Alexr. Chaplin & Co., Glasgow and London', pp. 21, 39, 53, 73 (Record Office for Leicestershire, Leicester and Rutland, ref 28D69/95). Number 346 is evidently out of sequence – other machines numbered in the mid-300s date from 1862 to 1863. The reason for this is not stated in the Register.
23. The rollers were numbered respectively 2016 and 2091 in Chaplin's 'Register of engines &c. manufactured and sold …' (see note 22), pp. 119, 123.
24. Cited in R. A. Whitehead, *A century of steam-rolling* (1975), p. 94.
25. Patent number 2986 of 24 October 1867; quote from patent specification, p. 4.
26. Entry for 'Steam-carriage', *Chambers's Encyclopaedia* (1868), vol. X, p. 742.
27. Patent number 401 of 13 February 1865.
28. J. Clydesdale, *Perth's first motor vehicle* (2004).
29. M. R. Lane, *The story of the St Nicholas Works: a history of Charles Burrell and Sons Limited 1803–1928* (1999), pp. 49–50.
30. Notes and bibliography on T. M. Tennant & Company in 'A–Z of Scottish engineering firms', Department of Science and Technology, National Museums Scotland; Commissioners of the International Exhibition of 1862, op. cit. (note 17), pp. 76–77. The numbers of road steamers built were provided by Tony Brown, road locomotive historian, personal communication, 26 February 2010.
31. *Transactions of the Highland and Agricultural Society of Scotland*, 4th series, vol. III (1871), Appendix A, 'Proceedings at General Meetings', p. 109.
32. Hughes (1972), op. cit. (note 14), pp. 114–19.
33. Lane (1999), op. cit. (note 29), p. 51.
34. 'Thomson road steamers by Robey & Co', unattributed list in steam vehicles file, Department of Science and Technology, National Museums Scotland.
35. J. Alexander, 'The Thomson road steamer in America', published at: www.steamtraction.com/article/2007-09-01 [accessed March 2011]
36. Fletcher (1891), op. cit., (note 4), pp. 180–82.

37. D. Tew, *Traction engines and the law* (1988), pp. 7–8.

38. *The Engineer*, 14 October 1870, p. 259; Fletcher (1891), op. cit. (note 4), pp. 182–84.

39. M. R. Lane, *The story of the Invicta Works: a history of Aveling and Porter, Rochester* (2010), pp. 4–19.

40. Ibid., pp. 14–16.

41. *Alexander Shanks and Sons, illustrated and descriptive catalogue* (undated, *c.*1876), p. 59; revised price list, September 1878, p. 59; catalogue (undated, *c.*1880) pp. 62–66; order book, 1882 (*e.g.* London order no. 326, December 1882); (Shanks archive, boxes 5 and 6, Signal Tower Museum, Arbroath).

42. Notes and bibliography on Bow McLachlan & Company in 'A–Z of Scottish engineering firms', Department of Science and Technology, National Museums Scotland.

43. *Engineering*, 29 January 1897, p. 140.

44. Tew (1988), op. cit. (note 37), pp. 8, 10.

45. P. G. Locke, 'The Bow McLachlan traction engine', in *The Road Locomotive Society Journal*, vol. 43, no. 2, May 1990, p. 54.

46. R. H. Clark, *The development of the English steam wagon* (1963), pp. 2–3. Despite its title, this work includes much technical information on Scottish-made steam wagons.

47. Ibid., pp. 32–33.

48. Ibid., pp. 9, 161.

49. K. A. Hurst, *William Beardmore: 'Transport is the thing'* (2004), pp. 9–12; Anon., 'The Thornycroft five-ton lorry', in *The Motor World*, 4 November 1905, pp. 1073–77.

50. Alley & MacLellan used the spelling 'waggon' rather than 'wagon' employed by other makers. For the sake of consistency, the latter spelling is used hereafter in describing their steam vehicles.

51. W. J. Hughes and J. L. Thomas, *'The Sentinel': vol. 1, 1875–1930* (1973), chs 1–4; A. R. and J. L. Thomas, *An album of 'Sentinel' works photographs: No. 1 Standards and Supers* (1992), pp. 10–19.

52. Hughes and Thomas (1973), op. cit. (note 51), p. 308; Thomas and Thomas (1992), op. cit. (note 51), pp. 21, 105–10.

53. Thomas and Thomas (1992), op. cit. (note 51), pp. 21–22.

Chapter 2

SELLING STEAM

SELLING STEAM

Presenting and Promoting Traction Engines

DURING the nineteenth and early twentieth centuries, the steam engine seemed to offer almost limitless power, suggesting that transport and agriculture could be practised in new ways. Manufacturers, merchants and other disciples were keen to convince potential users in town and country as to its possibilities. Then, as now, information about innovative technologies was gained and shared through trials and demonstrations, meetings and shows. These were arranged by local organisations and at a national level by the Highland and Agricultural Society of Scotland, which from the early nineteenth century encouraged improved practice in the rural industries. Within the industrial centres of Scotland, trade shows performed a similar role, such as the displays of vehicles at Scottish motor shows in the early twentieth century. Newspapers and magazines provided accounts of these events for those unable to witness them at first hand, with specialist publications such as *Transactions of the Highland and Agricultural Society of Scotland*, the weekly *North British Agriculturist*, and technical journals such as *The Engineer*, *Engineering*, *The Implement and Machinery Review*, and *The Motor World* reporting in greater detail. When steam technology became more settled, and the choice for purchasers of new equipment was between a large range of similar proven products, some English makers even adopted Scottish branding to try to make their machinery appeal to the local market.

Early field trials and demonstrations

The success of the steam locomotives used on railways during the 1830s and subsequent decades encouraged experimenters to believe that it should be possible to harness steam power for use on the land, not just for transport, but for cultivation and powering movable farm machinery too. A leading early exponent of investigation into steam power in agriculture was the Marquis of Tweeddale. Keen on utilising experiment and experience to evaluate the new technology, he suggested to the Highland and Agricultural Society of Scotland in 1834 that a prize should be made available for steam cultivation. Three years later a premium of £500 was offered by the Society. Steam ploughing was now in the Society's mind, and so a committee went to see a demonstration of Heathcote's steam plough in Lancashire. They were sufficiently impressed to have it brought to the Highland Show held at Dumfries in 1837, where it was the first steam plough to be seen in Scotland. Unfortunately, the demonstration was not a success and Heathcote's plough did not catch on. Despite the high value of the prize for steam ploughing, there were no contenders and in 1843 it was withdrawn. In 1851 and 1852 the Society offered another prize for a steam plough, but there was no winner until 1857 when John Fowler of Leeds satisfied the judges at a public trial in Stirling that their equipment worked well enough for £200 to be awarded.[1] Around this time the Highland Society's library was being added to with publications promoting the novel technology, such as *Progressive agriculture: a pamphlet on steam cultivation*[2] and *Fire and water versus corn and hay: an essay on the effects of steam cultivation*,[3] both by English authors. In 1864 the *Dundee Advertiser* published a booklet reprinting two recent articles describing more local experiences with steam ploughing.[4]

Meanwhile the practical Marquis of Tweeddale was also busy on his own account, trialling Fisken's and Fowler's steam cultivation equipment and comparing these with horse and ox ploughing on his estates in East Lothian. In addition to his role as President of the Highland and Agricultural Society, the Marquis also chaired the Society's Special Committee on Steam Cultivation, which was established in 1866. Membership included the eminent Professor W. J. Macquorn Rankine, the Society's consulting engineer, and Henry Stephens, author of the seminal textbook *Book of the farm*. That year, the committee visited six other farms in East Lothian and witnessed demonstrations of four different systems of cable ploughing, with steam engines powering various designs of winch for hauling the implements through the soil. Three of the farms used Fowler's system with single engine and self-acting anchor. Another used the roundabout system made by Howard of Bedford, powered by a portable steam engine made by Clayton & Shuttleworth of Lincoln. One farm used Coleman's system[5] and the last used Fowler's double-engine system. A range of implements were also in use, including ploughs, grubbers and cultivators. The committee's investigations lasted over three years and a detailed account of their findings regarding the benefits and drawbacks of steam cultivation was written up in the Society's *Transactions*. A recurring problem was the difficulty of collecting sufficient data to allow detailed comparison of the various systems and their costs.

In its summing up, the committee felt that Fowler's double-engine system was best suited to deep cultivation (around 12 to 14 inches), whilst Fowler's single-engine system and Howard's roundabout tackle were both suited to shallow work (eight inches or less). They made a qualified final judgment in favour of steam, stating …

on a large farm having a comparatively flat surface, with fields of not less than twenty acres, as nearly square as possible, and free from stones or other obstacles, and where three or four pairs of horses can be dispensed with, that steam cultivation will probably be highly beneficial as an auxiliary to horse power, as the work can be done with greater celerity and the ground cropped at the proper time, whereby an increased return would be likely to ensue.

Whilst large farms in the prosperous lowlands might be well placed to meet this ideal, they conceded that 'on a smaller extent of land there does not seem to be sufficient scope for the profitable employment of a steam plough'.[6] Put simply, steam was not going to replace the horse.

Another key point remained for debate, for there was by this time considerable interest in using a traction engine to haul the cultivating implement directly rather than by cable. To address this question, the Society resolved at its General Meeting in January 1870 to renew the Special Committee on Steam Cultivation, charging it with evaluating the use of Thomson's rubber-tyred road steamer for pulling a plough. No meeting was held by the committee during the following year, but at the Society's General Meeting in January 1871 the Earl of Dunmore was asked to provide an account of his recent experiences with his Thomson engines. The Earl felt that steam cultivation 'was in its infancy', but noted that the results of his trials had been sufficiently

Above:

FOWLER'S SINGLE ENGINE SYSTEM OF CULTIVATION, 1865

Fowler's single-engine system used a self-moving anchor at the opposite side of the field from the engine, and a reversible plough.

Below:

HOWARD'S SYSTEM OF CULTIVATION, 1865

This system used a windlass powered by a portable steam engine to haul the plough.

(© Both images: National Museums Scotland; source, *Chambers's Encyclopaedia* [1865], vol. vii, pp. 606, 607)

ROAD STEAMER OWNED BY THE EARL OF DUNMORE, AIRTH, 1870

The Earl of Dunmore's road steamer with vertical engine hauling a double-ended plough at Airth, Stirlingshire, 1870.

During the last summer he [Lord Dunmore] had built a new engine of eight-horse-power. Those he had were on a different principle from most of Thomson's, because the original ones [engines] were horizontal. The last one he had was vertical, and he found it answered better for the work, and was more economical, as it could be worked by only a man and a boy, instead of two skilled men.[9]

(© National Museums Scotland, SLA C25965)

encouraging to greatly impress one of the partners of the leading English agricultural engineering firm Ransomes, Sims & Head, as recounted in the previous chapter.[7] Shortly afterwards, the *Scotsman* reprinted an article from *The Engineer* advocating full-scale experiment to establish the practicability of direct ploughing using traction engines like Thomson's road steamer. The article struggled to be even-handed and indulged in caricature to describe the virtues of the traction engine over the large and heavy cable ploughing engine, which could only 'drag its unwieldiness from place to place, slowly and painfully, on good roads; but it is as different from the true road locomotive as a hippopotamus is from a gazelle'.[8]

Despite such passion, few others were persuaded to try direct ploughing by steam. In those instances where steam power was used for cultivation in Scotland, Fowler's powerful double-engine cable system went on to prevail almost totally. In April 1872, John Gordon arranged for a demonstration of this equipment, owned by the Scottish Steam Cultivation and Traction Company (which we will learn more about in the next chapter), for his tenant farmers at Slains in Aberdeenshire. There the soil was heavy clay, making it hard work for horse ploughing. A huge audience – more than a thousand people – attended the trial, and when it was complete John Gordon hosted a dinner attended by two hundred, including his tenants.[10]

The power of the model

Just as Symington in 1786 and Nasmyth in 1827 used models to demonstrate their steam carriage designs, so too did agricultural inventors sometimes exploit miniatures, allowing their thinking to be brought right into the city before meetings of learned bodies like the British Association for the Advancement of Science, and the Highland and Agricultural Society (which gathered together a remarkable range of model cultivating implements in its Edinburgh premises).

At the British Association's meeting in Edinburgh in August 1850, James Usher was able to demonstrate the principles of his recently-patented steam digger using a working model. The model was shown again at the Great Exhibition in 1851, and a full size version was made by Slight of Edinburgh and demonstrated publicly at Inverleith. The invention aroused considerable interest: it was given an award by the Highland and Agricultural Society in 1852, and described and illustrated in important engineering texts of the time. In one of these, a nautical analogy was used to describe the operation of the digger:

Another expedient is to have revolving ploughshares set on an axle, driven by a locomotive engine, which is slowly advanced by the ploughshares biting the ground, in the manner a steam vessel is propelled by paddle wheels.

Two further machines were made in 1853 and 1854. Nonetheless the digger failed to find lasting success as it could not cope with a variety of soils.[11]

JAMES USHER'S STEAM DIGGER, 1850

Model of James Usher's steam digger, demonstrated at the British Association meeting in Edinburgh in 1850.

(© Science Museum/SSPL)

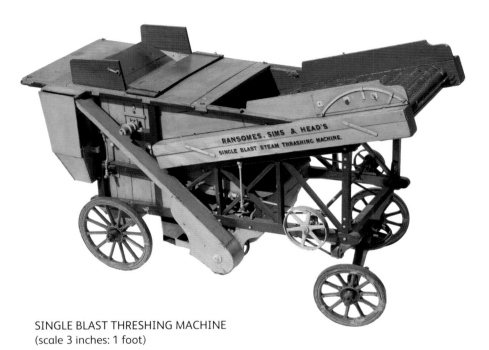

SINGLE BLAST THRESHING MACHINE
(scale 3 inches: 1 foot)

This working model was bought by Edinburgh Museum of Science & Art (National Museums Scotland) in November 1879 from Ransomes, Sims & Head, Ipswich, as an example of the latest design of mobile threshing machine intended to be powered by a portable or traction engine.

(© National Museums Scotland, T.1879.50)

Scientific tests and trials

In 1876 Fisken of Leeds used a model at the Highland and Agricultural Society's summer show in Aberdeen to demonstrate their improved design of steam cultivating machinery. The model impressed the Implement Committee sufficiently to inspire the Society to embark on a thorough trial of Fisken's full-size system. Professor Macquorn Rankine had died four years previously, but his practical and instructive approach to engineering was now thoroughly embedded in the work of the Society. The trial took place on three farms near Edinburgh over five days the following November. Fisken's system was another which used cable to move the implement, and was powered by a single steam engine, in this instance Robey's patent 10-horsepower traction engine. The plough used was Fisken's three furrow patent, and an Easton and Amos dynamometer provided an accurate measure of the power required to haul the plough. The engine's speed, its consumption of coal and water, and the time taken to set up the tackle, were all measured. With so much data collected, this was one of the most comprehensive trials yet carried out in Scotland. The published report concluded:

The application of steam-power to the tillage of the soil is pre-eminently one of those subjects which, from its importance, the Committee think should be fully investigated, in order that agriculturists may be provided with authoritative data for their guidance in selecting the implements they employ; and following-out this view, they are of

[the] *opinion that every inventor who claims superiority for his system of steam tillage should be encouraged by the Society to submit it to a trial similar to that afforded by Messrs Fisken …*

Fisken were awarded a premium of 50 guineas by the Society for the satisfactory performance of their apparatus during the trial.[12]

This same spirit of scientific investigation informed the competitions for machines and implements held at some of the Highland and Agricultural Society's annual shows. At the Glasgow Show in 1888, a premium of £75 was offered for 'the best fixed Steam Engine, with boiler combined or separate, for erection in steadings, to drive all ordinary farm machinery, nominal power six-horse'. Points were allocated to eight items, including price, simplicity of design and operation, economy of fuel, water and lubricating oil (all of which were measured carefully), and regularity of speed. The power output was measured with a friction brake borrowed from the Royal Agricultural Society of England, an indication that this sort of technical trial was a new venture for the Highland Society. Six engines were entered, but only four were tested, two English and two Scottish. One was a portable engine made by McLaren of Leeds; the others were stationary boilers and engines by Foden of Sandbach in Cheshire, Hogarth of Kelso, and Young of Ardrossan. The report of the trial, which was published in the Society's *Transactions*, included a level of technical detail (including reproductions of the steam engine indicator diagrams and Moscrop recordings of steam

pressure and engine speed) which would not have been out of place in a mechanical engineering journal. The prize was awarded to McLaren's portable engine with 86 out of 100 points. Foden, Hogarth and Young scored 66, 56, and 43 points respectively.[13]

The next such event, although non-competitive, was the trial of ten stationary oil-fuel engines at the Edinburgh Show in 1899. Here power output, fuel consumption and thermal efficiency were measured and compared, and reported in detail in the Society's *Transactions*.[14] At the Glasgow Show in 1905 there was another non-competitive trial run along the same lines, for gas engines fuelled by an attached gas producer plant.[15]

Tractor trials

The Highland Society did not carry out any similarly detailed tests on traction engines, but it did carry out a number of trials of farm tractors, two of which included a traction engine. These tractor trials were conceived of more as educational demonstrations, like the steam cultivation trials of the 1860s, rather than full-blown technical trials. The first of these was the 'Exhibition Trial' of tractors at Stirling in 1915. Although wartime conditions made it difficult to organise this event, the Society nevertheless considered that shortages of men and horses for agricultural work made it vital. Entrants were assessed for the quality of their design and construction, ease of use and quality of work, and fuel consumption. Seven tractors entered, of which five were

especially prepared for display at the show, painted in bright colours, their metalwork polished and woodwork varnished, all to a high state of gloss. The show regulations stated that 'All machines requiring steam or fire' had to burn coke. A penalty of £5 would be incurred for burning coal,[23] to ensure there was no nuisance from smoke. Imagining further, we can sense the sharp smell of coke fumes, the chuffing sound of gas and oil engine exhausts, the rhythmic puffing of steam engines, the slap of moving leather belts and hum of whirring machinery.

Not all the equipment displayed at such shows was necessarily purchased there and put into use straight away. Some had already been ordered and so manufacturers were taking advantage of the show to display items en route to their new owners, ideally winning more orders in the process. For those machines not collected by their owners straight from the showground some would have been delivered subsequently, perhaps after being exhibited again at a smaller, local agricultural show. Manufacturers were of course happy to sell items from the display stock, with the attraction for the purchaser of then getting a show-finished machine at no extra cost. Exhibitors would have been very happy to take an order for something already sold, or not on display, but illustrated in a sales brochure or advertisement. At the end of the Show, unsold products were taken back to the factory and readied again for display at another show.

The official catalogue of implements exhibited at the 1907 Show provides a detailed insight into the range of powered vehicles and engines then available to Scottish farmers, contractors and hauliers. Sixteen businesses entered a total of 31 steam engines: 15 traction engines; six steam wagons; four steam tractors; two road locomotives; two road rollers; and two portable steam engines. There were two oil engine tractors, but no other motor vehicles.[24] Most of the traction engine manufacturers showed one or two machines, including Fowler and McLaren who both showed a traction engine and a larger engine for haulage. Some, such as Ransomes, Sims & Jefferies of Ipswich also showed implements and threshing machines. (English makers used the term 'threshing' or 'thrashing machine' to describe their products, whilst the Scots favoured the term 'threshing mill'.) Marshall, Sons & Company of Gainsborough had indicated that they would present two traction engines (one of 6-horsepower and one of 7-horsepower) and three 'thrashing machines', but in the event only the smaller traction engine appeared, accompanied by four machines.[25]

Robey of Lincoln showed four machines: traction engine, road locomotive, steam wagon and steam tractor. Aveling & Porter also had four entries: steam tractor, traction engine and two steam rollers. One of these, a 'Steam Road Roller, original type, as manufactured between 1865 and 1870', was not for sale. It must have made an interesting exhibit, intended no doubt to underline Aveling's pre-eminent place in the history of the industry.[26] Two of the six steam wagons were from Scottish manufacturers: Alley & MacLellan's Sentinel, and one by D. Stewart of Glasgow.

ADVERTISEMENTS

ADVERTISEMENTS BY
RANSOMES, SIMS & JEFFERIES
and MARSHALL, SONS &
COMPANY, 1907

(© National Museums Scotland;
source, *North British Agriculturalist*,
July 1907)

HIGHLAND SHOW, STAND No. 219.

Appointed by Royal Warrant Manufacturers of Agricultural Machinery to His Majesty KING EDWARD VII.

RANSOMES, SIMS & JEFFERIES
LIMITED

Are Exhibiting at the HIGHLAND SHOW at EDINBURGH

A Newly-designed 6 N.H.P. Compound Traction Engine, also

A 7 Horse-Power Nominal Traction Engine and

2 54-inch Finishing Thrashing Machines;

ALSO A LARGE SELECTION OF THEIR

CELEBRATED PLOUGHS FOR SCOTLAND,

"IPSWICH" STEEL CULTIVATORS,

ROTARY POTATO DIGGERS and HORSE RAKES.

Complete Illustrated Catalogues free on application either at the Stand or direct to the

ORWELL WORKS, IPSWICH.

FOR

THE LATEST in Steam THRASHING MACHINERY
CALL AT

MARSHALL, SONS & CO.'S STAND, No. 202.

At the HIGHLAND SOCIETY'S SHOW, to be held at EDINBURGH, JULY 9th to 12th.

WHERE THEY WILL EXHIBIT THEIR LATEST

TRACTION ENGINES
AND

FOUR FINISHING THRASHING MILLS,
WITH ALL THE LATEST IMPROVEMENTS.

TRACTION ENGINES.

THRASHING MACHINERY.

M., S., & Co. have very Extensive Manufacturing Facilities, replete with all the Most Modern Machine Tools and Appliances for turning out High class Work in every Department, but Customers are requested to intimate their requirements as early as possible to prevent disappointment in delivery.

N.B.—UPWARDS OF 120,000 ENGINES, MACHINES, &c., MADE AND SENT OUT FROM THE BRITANNIA WORKS, GAINSBOROUGH.

Selling steam at the Motor Show

The Scottish Motor Show held the previous year in Glasgow provided a similar showcase, not only for automobiles but also commercial vehicles. Nine steam wagons were exhibited, with the following Scottish makes represented – the Glasgow Motor Lorry Company, Robert Morton & Sons of Wishaw, and D. Stewart of Glasgow. Surprisingly there was no Sentinel wagon. English manufacturers present were T. Coulthard & Company Limited, Preston, and the Yorkshire Patent Steam Wagon Company of Leeds.[27]

Marketing the English traction engine to Scotland

Some English firms made special efforts to identify their products with Scottish buyers. Between 1905 and 1909 Charles Burrell of Thetford produced a small, 6-horse-power traction engine and branded it 'The Aberdeenshire Engine' on the polished cast-iron nameplate attached to the smokebox door. Nine were made, but only three were sold into Scotland,[28] which was hardly a marketing success. Sometimes sales literature was prepared with Scottish content. Marshall's catalogue of December 1918 includes a full-page photograph of an attractively painted traction engine and threshing machine 'at work in Scotland', in an idealised scene on

TWO STEWART-THORNYCROFT STEAM WAGONS, 1906

As displayed at the Scottish Motor Show, Glasgow, March 1906. Both are fitted with tipping bodies.

(© National Museums Scotland; source, *The Motor World*, 17 March 1906, p. 259)

51

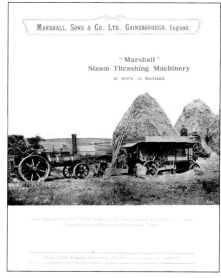

MARSHALL, SONS & CO., LTD., GAINSBOROUGH, England.

"Marshall"
Steam Thrashing Machinery
at work in Scotland.

Left:

FODEN 5-TON STEAM WAGON, 1924

Colour advertising post-card of Foden steam wagon no. 11280, painted in Balmoral livery

(© Mortons Archive)

Right:

STEAM THRESHING IN SCOTLAND

Marshall catalogue, 1918, p. 35.

(© National Museums Scotland)

what appears to be a bright and sunny day.[29] A Fowler steam roller catalogue includes testimonials from the county surveyors in East Lothian and Aberdeenshire written in 1925, and a list of users of Fowler road rollers which included eleven Scottish councils.[30] On a smaller scale, Foden produced a colour postcard of a new steam wagon working at Balmoral.

Black and white photographs and catalogue illustrations were however more usual in this period, making it difficult to see the colourful and attractive liveries applied to most traction engines. For example, Burrell and Marshall typically wore rich reds and greens, with Fowler and McLaren favouring black set off with contrasting lining. Some makers added a large transfer to each side of the engine, often with representations of prize medals won. In McLaren's case their transfers

included the gold medal awarded to them at the Highland Show in Dumfries in 1878 for their 'Improved Traction Engine', and their last design of transfer (c.1911) included reference to the prize from the Highland and Agricultural Society for their portable steam engine exhibited at the Glasgow Show in 1888.

Leeds-based J. & H. McLaren made much of their Scottish ancestry in creating what today would be recognised as their brand image. The McLaren family had originally come from Perthshire, and although the firm's founders (brothers John and Henry McLaren) were born in England near Sunderland[31] they were evidently so proud of their clan ties with Scotland that they used the ancient Royal Arms of Scotland on the cover and title page of some of their sales literature. The Scottish connection was further highlighted inside their catalogues. The 1910 issue opened by noting that the business was established in 1876 and 'No. 1 Engine, of 12 H.P. (nominal) was sent out of our works on 20th March, 1877. It is still working satisfactorily in the North of Scotland.' This was repeated in the 1914 issue.[32] Reproductions of medals from the Highland Society and East Lothian Agricultural Society were included too amongst representations of prizes awarded across the globe.

McLAREN TRACTION ENGINE

Maker's photograph of a new McLaren traction engine, showing the decorative transfer on the side of the boiler lagging. The transfer had representations of some of the prize medals won by McLaren, including the gold medal awarded at the Highland Show in Dumfries in 1878 for their traction engine.

This photograph hung in the office of John Turnbull of Chirnside, Berwickshire. Turnbull was a good customer for McLaren: he purchased five such engines for his threshing and haulage business between 1894 and 1903.

(© National Museums Scotland, SLA C25924)

J. & H. McLAREN

Catalogues

Left: McLAREN CATALOGUE, 1908

Left: McLAREN CATALOGUE, 1908

Cover of McLaren steam ploughing catalogue no. 17 of 1908, with the Royal Arms of Scotland prominently displayed.

(© Museum of English Rural Life, University of Reading)

Below: McLAREN CATALOGUE, 1910

McLaren 1910 catalogue medal pages showing Scottish awards.

(Alexander Hayward)

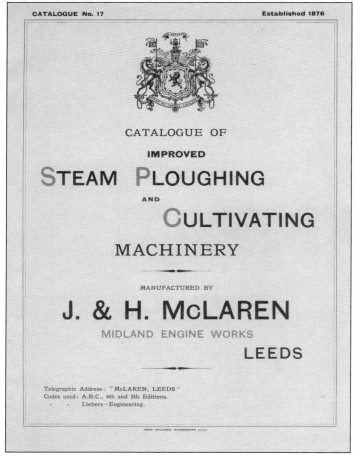

How far this tactic was successful in winning Scottish customers is debatable. McLaren was in fact one of the smaller English traction engine manufacturers, operating towards the upper end of the market, making it difficult to compare its marketing success against other, more prolific, competitors like Burrell and Fowler. Nevertheless, over the years their products did find some success in Scotland, ranging from single purchases like the 8-horse power engine bought for the Duke of Roxburgh's large estate near Kelso, to the five machines bought by contractor John Turnbull of Chirnside.[33] It is worth noting in conclusion that McLaren exported much of their production overseas, so their catalogues were no doubt seen by some diaspora Scots farming in Africa, Australia, New Zealand and South America. We shall never know how far their choices in machinery were shaped by McLaren's appeals to their own sense of Scottishness.

References

1. Highland and Agricultural Society of Scotland, *Report on the present state of the agriculture of Scotland* (1878), pp. 149-50.
2. J. A. Williams, *Progressive agriculture: a pamphlet on steam cultivation* (1858).
3. S. Hutchinson, *Fire and water versus corn and hay: an essay on the effects of steam cultivation* (1863).
4. Anon., *Lord Kinnaird's model farm: a visit to Millhill* [and] *The steam plough in the Carse of Gowrie* (1864).
5. It is likely that the system referred to was made by Coleman & Morton of Chelmsford, Essex, who commenced in 1862 with a specially adapted traction engine with winches mounted on the side of the boiler. In 1864 they developed a twin engine system. Both are described in C. Tyler and J. Haining, *Ploughing by steam* (1970), pp. 102–104.
6. Marquis of Tweeddale, 'Report of special committee of the Highland and Agricultural Society of Scotland appointed to inspect and report on the various systems of cultivating land by steam power in East Lothian', *Transactions of the Highland and Agricultural Society of Scotland*, 4th series, vol. III, 1871, pp. 274–90 (quotations from p. 289).
7. Ibid., Appendix A, 'Proceedings at General Meetings', pp. 108–110 (quote from p. 109).
8. The *Scotsman*, 24 February 1871, p. 8.
9. Marquis of Tweeddale, op. cit. (note 6), p. 109.
10. J. Cruickshank, *Changes in the agricultural industry of Aberdeenshire in the last fifty years* (1935), p. 4.
11. *Civil Engineer and Architect's Journal*, vol. XIII, 1850, pp. 329–31; *The British Farmer's Magazine*, 1851, pp. 487–88; Highland and Agricultural Society of Scotland (1878), op. cit. (note 1), p. 150; J. Bourne, *A catechism of the steam engine* (1856), pp. 492–95; C. Tyler, *Digging by steam* (1977), pp. 139–43. Quote from Bourne, pp. 492–93.
12. Anon., 'On implements selected for trial: Part 1 Fisken steam cultivating machinery', *Transactions of the Highland and Agricultural Society of Scotland*, 4th series, vol. IX, 1877, pp. 324–33 (quote from p. 333).
13. J. S. Dudgeon, A. S. Logan, J. Middleton and J. T. S. Paterson, 'Report of the trials of steam engines at Glasgow 1888, by the judges', *Transactions of the Highland and Agricultural Society of Scotland*, 5th series, vol. I, 1889, pp. 123–31 (quote from p. 123).
14. Anon., 'Trial of oil-engines', *Transactions of the Highland and Agricultural Society of Scotland*, 5th series, vol. XII, 1900, pp. 388–408.
15. Anon., 'Trials of suction gas-producer plants', *Transactions of the Highland and Agricultural Society of Scotland*, 5th series, vol. XVIII, 1906, pp. 208–23.
16. *Highland and Agricultural Society of Scotland, Exhibition trial of motor tillage implements*, 1915, pp. 1–9 (quotation from p. 9).
17. B. Kennedy, *Demonstrations and trials of tractors 1904–1934* (Reprints from the trial

reports in contemporary volumes of *Trans-actions of the Highland and Agricultural Society of Scotland* [1990]).

18. J. D. G. Davidson (ed.), *A short history: 1784–1984, Royal Highland and Agricultural Society of Scotland* (1984), p. 56–57.
19. The *Scotsman*, 9 July 1907, p. 5.
20. Anon., 'Trials of agricultural motors and dung-distributors', *Transactions of the Highland and Agricultural Society of Scotland*, 5th series, vol. XVII, 1905, p. 427.
21. *Highland and Agricultural Society of Scotland, Implement catalogue: Edinburgh Show*, 1907.
22. The *Scotsman*, 9 July 1907 (note 19).
23. *Transactions of the Highland and Agricultural Society of Scotland*, 5th series, vol. XIX, 1907, Appendix A, 'Regulations for General Show at Edinburgh', p. 64.
24. *Highland and Agricultural Society of Scotland* (1907), op. cit. (note 21), pp. 91–119.
25. Ibid., p. 103; *The North British Agriculturist*, 11 July 1907, p. 443.
26. *Highland and Agricultural Society of Scotland* (1907), op. cit. (note 21), pp. 114–15. Aveling & Porter's steam tractor was catalogued as a 'Compound Motor Tractor', because it was designed to comply with the recent Heavy Motor Car regulations of 1904.
27. Anon., 'The Glasgow show', *The Motor World*, 17 March 1906, pp. 251–59.
28. G. F. A. Gilbert and D. J. Osborne, *Charles Burrell & Sons Ltd* (n.d.), p. 26.
29. *Marshall, Sons and Company, Agricultural engines and machinery*, publication no. 1048 (Gainsborough, 1918), p. 35.
30. *John Fowler and Company (Leeds) Limited, Road making machinery* (facsimile published by the Road Locomotive Society, n.d.), pp. 8, 18, 23.
31. J. Pease, *The history of J and H McLaren of Leeds* (2003), pp. 7–8.
32. J and H. McLaren, *Catalogue of traction engines … etc.* (1910), p. 7; *Catalogue of traction engines … etc.* (1914), p. 4. Pease, op. cit. (note 31), p. 18, observes that McLaren traction engine no. 1 was sold to Bell & Company in Arbroath, and that William Bell was John and Henry McLaren's cousin.
33. Alan Duke engine lists for Berwickshire and Roxburghshire, held by the Road Locomotive Society.

Chapter 3

WORKING WITH STEAM

WORKING WITH STEAM

Uses and Users of Traction Engines

THE traction engine in its various forms had three main uses in Scotland: threshing, road haulage and road making, with a smaller number used for cultivation. Because of the high first cost of this equipment, ownership was generally restricted to wealthy landowners, or local contractors and large enterprises who kept it employed by hiring it out. Such machinery and those associated with it were often of interest to contemporary photographers, as can be seen in many of the images selected to illustrate this chapter. Not only do these demonstrate the form and purpose of the machinery, they also reveal something of peoples' relationship with it. Whether in the pioneering days of the Victorian period, or in the mid-twentieth century by which time steam was nearing the end of the road, workers often stand proudly alongside the equipment they are operating, or a fascinated audience watches as some huge load is hauled by. Both in the towns and cities where steam was commonplace, or in rural Scotland where it only occasionally intruded, the traction engine served, like a passing train, to remind people they were part of the Age of Steam.

Origins: the portable engine

Our survey begins with the portable steam engine. This not only provided a basis for the development of the self-moving traction engine, but had a long history of use in its own right as a simple, easily movable source of power for machinery on the farm and rural factory. The portable engine consisted simply of an engine fitted onto a boiler, the whole mounted on travelling wheels so it could be towed to its workplace, usually by horse. In Scotland a notable application was in forestry, with large portable engines powering sawmills during both World Wars as Britain sought to become self-sufficient in timber production. The very last portable engines manufactured in the 1940s for the British market by Marshall of Gainsborough and Foster of Lincoln were used in this way, and were fitted with extra large fireboxes so that they could use waste wood from the mill as fuel.

Simple machine: the traction engine defined

The basic design of the traction engine was largely settled by 1880, with the usual form consisting of a locomotive type boiler carrying the engine which drove the rear wheels through a train of gears.[1] Traction engines typically had a single cylinder for mechanical simplicity, although sometimes two cylinders were fitted. In this case the cylinders were usually arranged on the compound principle, where the exhaust steam from one cylinder was reused in another slightly larger cylinder. Compound traction engines therefore used less coal and water and ran more smoothly and with a softer exhaust than a single-cylinder engine, but had many more moving parts to lubricate and adjust, and were more expensive to purchase. When stationary, the engine could be used to power machinery like a threshing mill, saw bench or stone crusher by belt from its flywheel, and a governor was fitted to ensure that it ran this at a steady speed. Two speeds were generally fitted for travelling on the road, nominally two and four miles per hour, the latter being the legal maximum under the Locomotives Act of 1865. When being used for haulage, the typical traction engine could pull around 15 tons, but sometimes much heavier loads were attempted. The full description for such machines is agricultural, or general purpose, traction engine. Because of their suitability for many tasks, they were found over much of lowland Scotland: from the farms in the south-west, across the central belt from Glasgow to Edinburgh, along the arable east coast from Berwickshire in the south to Caithness in the far north, and over the Pentland Firth to Orkney.

This chapter now considers the various adaptations and applications of the basic traction engine design for different tasks: ploughing, threshing, hauling and road rolling.

HORSE-DRAWN PLOUGH, 1928

Horse-power was used for the bulk of cultivation in Scotland long after the introduction of steam ploughing, continuing in some instances until the 1950s when replaced by the tractor. Here ploughman Alex Cowan is working with two Clydesdale horses pulling an iron-framed plough at Bridgehouse, Westfield, West Lothian in 1928.

(© National Museums Scotland, SLA W501216)

GENERAL PURPOSE ENGINE

A general purpose traction engine at a sawmill near Dunkeld, Perthshire, c.1900.

The driving belt from the engine's flywheel is connected to a saw bench with a large circular saw blade (behind the group on the left). The horse on the right is hitched to a cart carrying a large barrel of water for the engine. The machinery has been stopped and everyone has paused for the photographer.

(© National Museums Scotland, Scottish Life Archive)

Ploughing

Cultivation

Steam cultivation represents the earliest use of the traction engine in Scotland, although even after its promotion by opinion-formers such as the Marquis of Tweeddale around the middle of the nineteenth century, and the allied efforts of inventors and entrepreneurs, it still remained relatively uncommon. In 1878 the Highland and Agricultural Society reported:

> Although much may be expected from steam power, as applied to the culture of the soil, Scotch farmers do not generally appear to be much enamoured of it. They have still to be convinced that much saving can thereby be effected, as compared with horse power. The one-furrow swing plough, drawn by two horses, still turns over the great bulk of the land in Scotland, while two-horse grubbers and harrows cultivate it. Probably not more than fifty sets of steam ploughing tackle are to be found in Scotland.[2]

These fifty sets of tackle would have comprised all the systems then in use, such as Fowler's near-ubiquitous double-engine system, the single-engine system with a self-moving anchor, those using a stationary windlass powered by either a portable engine or traction engine, and maybe even a few examples of direct ploughing using a traction engine hauling the plough directly, as with Thomson's road steamers mentioned previously.

Since steam ploughing tackle was often used on more than one location, these various sets would have worked on some hundreds of farms.

Indeed, the fact that steam cultivation had spread at all through suitable areas of Scotland in the 1860s and 1870s owed much to a number of companies established with the aim of making it widely available to farmers. This was the era of High Farming, when the application of science and technology to agriculture (made viable by high crop prices) promised increased productivity. The first such company to be established was in Kincardineshire in 1866, one of the leaders of this enterprise being George Greig who ran a large farm at Harvieston. His brother David had a mechanical bent and worked with John Fowler of Leeds from 1855. The two Greig brothers became intimately involved with the Fowler firm: David becoming a partner, and George an agent for Fowler's products in north-east Scotland. Both brothers were patentees of some of the equipment produced by Fowler, David in particular having a large involvement in the technical side of the business. Inevitably the Kincardineshire Steam Ploughing Company used Fowler's double-engine system (they had two sets), setting an example which subsequent cultivating companies were to follow.[3]

The Kincardineshire company was soon paying handsome dividends and inspiring imitators. In Edinburgh the Scottish Steam Cultivation & Traction Company was launched in 1871 under the chairmanship of the Earl of Dunmore, with the intention of raising £50,000 capital and placing …

DOUBLE-ENGINE STEAM PLOUGHING

**A PAIR OF PLOUGHING ENGINES
AT WORK, WITH DOUBLE-ENDED
PLOUGH**

This illustration shows how steam ploughing was
best suited to rectangular fields. It is taken from
Stephens' book of the farm (1908), vol. 1, p. 424,
fig. 331.

Below:

FOWLER DOUBLE-ENDED 4-FURROW BALANCE PLOUGH

This was first developed for use with Fowler's single-engine system, but the same design was then used in double-engine ploughing. At the end of each furrow, the plough-man dismounted, pulled the raised beam and ploughshares down onto the soil, climbed back on and steered the plough back to the other side of the field. The illustration comes from *Chambers's Encyclopaedia* (1865), vol. vii, p. 606, fig. 11.

(© National Museums Scotland)

With this system two ploughing engines were used, each located at opposite sides of a field. These were essentially general purpose traction engines fitted with a powered winch (termed a 'winding drum') which held a long length of wire cable attached to the implement (typically a double-ended balance plough, or a cultivator), allowing it to be hauled to and fro across the field. After each pull, the engine moved up the field by the width of the implement, ready to pull it back on unbroken soil when it reached the far side of the field.

The double-engine system was mechanically simple and typically the equipment used was larger and more robust than the various single-engine systems with their windlass, fixed and moving anchors, rope porters and other paraphernalia. One drawback however was that two engine drivers were needed, and likewise twice the quantity of fuel and water was used in comparison with single-engine systems. As with other cable ploughing systems, the ploughing engines were stationary whilst pulling the implement. This allowed them to transmit all their power to the implement, unlike tractor-hauled ploughing where some of the tractor's power is absorbed in propelling itself along the field. There was also the advantage that the great weight of the ploughing engine was kept off the land to be cultivated, reducing soil compaction.

A large set of double-engine tackle could work up to 16 acres per day with a 6-furrow plough, or 25 acres per day when using an 11-tine cultivator. In contrast, a single-furrow horse plough could cover around an acre a day.[4]

steam cultivation within the reach of the tenant farmer, be he a large holder or a small one, and to enable him thus to do with cheapness and rapidity the work he had hitherto done expensively and slowly, and at the same time lessen his yearly expenditure in horseflesh and keep. Believing that such a company as this would confer great benefits on agriculture, and that it could hardly fail to be a success commercially …,

the company set about equipping itself for a range of stations in the Carse of Gowrie, Stirling and Roxburghshire. The setting up of further stations in Aberdeen, Banff, East Lothian, Selkirk and Wigtownshire was to be dependent on the availability of new steam ploughing tackle, and the number of shareholders in each district.[5] By April 1872 the company had a large set of Fowler tackle (two 12-horsepower ploughing engines, a 4-furrow balance plough, 9-tine cultivator and set of harrows) at work at Slains in Aberdeenshire. Soon the newly established Philorth Steam Cultivation & Traction Company took over there with a similar set of Fowler tackle. For the next few years hundreds of acres were ploughed and business was good, though income for all the companies fell away as the decade advanced. Their charges were based on servicing the tackle's high capital costs and paying for the skilled labour required for its operation, making its use comparatively costly. The early optimism about the inevitable commercial success of steam cultivation was soon shown to be misplaced when grain prices fell and the ensuing agricultural depression

rendered its use uneconomical. The result was that farmers returned to what they knew best and could afford, *i.e.* horse ploughing. The Scottish (Edinburgh) company was wound up in 1881, followed by the Kincardineshire company in 1885 and Philorth company in 1888.[6]

Steam ploughing tackle when well maintained could last for several decades, and with only a dozen or so seasons' use the cultivation companies' equipment would have been fit for selling on for further work. Andrew Gilchrist was one of those who remained a keen exponent of the steam plough. He introduced steam cultivation to Fife in 1868, subsequently becoming manager of the Fife section of the Scottish Steam Cultivation & Traction Company, and kept some Fowler double-engine tackle in use on his large farms until his death in 1911. Among a number of innovations, Gilchrist devised a means of ploughing, sowing and harrowing by steam in a single operation.[7]

A map prepared by John Fowler & Company in 1918 recorded only four sets of steam ploughing tackle in use in Scotland (two in East Lothian and one each in Berwickshire and Roxburghshire), and very few sets of tackle were added after the First World War. A pair of new small (10-horsepower) Fowler engines was delivered in 1925 and registered for the road in Kincardineshire, and a pair of 14-horsepower Fowler engines was delivered in the same year and registered for use in Ayrshire. By 1937 the smaller pair was in Cupar, Fife, being then the last set of steam ploughing tackle at work in Scotland.[8]

Above:

ANDREW GILCHRIST J.P. (1832–1911), TAKEN IN *c*.1890

Gilchrist farmed at Carvenom, near Anstruther, East Fife. His interests extended beyond farming to supporting many local organisations including the parish council, church, school and hospital. Gilchrist employed not only steam ploughs, but was also proud of the work-horses used on his farm.

(© National Museums Scotland, SLA W511105A)

Below:

GILCHRIST'S FOWLER SINGLE-CYLINDER PLOUGHING ENGINE (side view)

Andrew Gilchrist's pair of Fowler ploughing engines were made in 1869 (builder's numbers 1145 and 1149). The long lever above the rear wheel controls the clutch which engages and disengages the drive from the engine to the winding drum. The attractively curved safety-valve cover on top of the cylinder and steering wheel mounted on a vertical shaft at the rear of the engine, are features typical of early Fowler ploughing engines. This photograph dates from 1911 and shows the engine, now around 40 years old, clean and still well maintained.

(© National Museums Scotland, SLA C13250)

STEAM PLOUGHING IN FIFE

Above (left):

FOWLER BALANCE PLOUGH

A Fowler balance plough in use at Carvenom, *c.*1911. The ploughman is holding the steering wheel, and the two handles above the wheels (linked by a chain to prevent them turning whilst at work) were used by him to adjust the depth of ploughing.

(© National Museums Scotland, SLA W504405)

Above (right):

FARM WORKERS AT CARVENOM, c.1912

This photograph was taken shortly after Andrew Gilchrist's death, as his family were preparing to leave the farm, *c.*1912. The men at each end of the front bench had looked after the steam engines for the preceding forty years. David Ross, chief engineer, is seated on the left and John Robertson, second engineer, is on the right.

(© National Museums Scotland, SLA W511113A)

Below:

ON THE ROAD

A set of Fowler double-engine steam ploughing tackle on the road near Markinch, Fife, *c.*1880. The leading engine is towing a Fowler living van which provided accommodation for the ploughing crew when away from home. The implement is out of sight behind the second engine.

(© National Museums Scotland, SLA C13249)

Left:

ENVELOPE FROM JOHN FOWLER & COMPANY

Envelope from John Fowler & Company in Leeds addressed to Andrew Gilchrist, Carvenom, postmarked 23 November 1907. Fowler have used the envelope to advertise their products of the time; the bottom illustration (see detail) shows a large ploughing engine with compound cylinders which can be contrasted with Gilchrist's much older machines.

(© National Museums Scotland, W.MS.1985.52.1)

Right:

BOAT-HAULING AT ST MONANCE

Ploughing engines could also be used for hauling heavy loads. Here a fishing boat is being moved from a boat-builder's yard at St Monance on the Fife coast. The Fowler engine was probably owned by Andrew Gilchrist.

(© National Museums Scotland, SLA 20/06/12)

Land Reclamation

Steam ploughing engines could also be used for land reclamation. The largest such scheme in Britain was undertaken in the 1870s by the third Duke of Sutherland, a wealthy enthusiast for steam power who saw in it the means of helping claim the peat bogs and moorland of Sutherland for agriculture. In so doing, the Duke aimed to provide the conditions necessary for the county to become self sufficient in the production of oats for the human population and turnips as winter feed for sheep, with a commensurate increase in the Sutherland estate's rental value.[9]

Work got underway on the principal site in 1872 near Lairg at the southern end of Loch Shin. At first an old set of Howard steam-powered windlass tackle was employed (it had been used previously to reclaim a small area of land at Uppat), but it was unable to cope with the large buried stones and tree roots encountered. In its place a battery of more powerful Fowler equipment was introduced in 1873.

When the operations were in full force no fewer than fourteen steam engines were 'puffing away' at one time, and several hundred workmen and many horses busily employed. Drainage, ploughing, clearing off stones, harrowing, erecting fences, making roads, building houses, were all in progress at once, creating a stir and bustle which, in a valley hemmed in by hills on all sides, could not have failed to impress the visitor as marvellous.

Over 1800 acres was reclaimed for arable use at Loch Shin over four years. No sooner had these works finished than work started on a similar scheme at Kildonan in 1877. Three years later nearly 500 acres was available for cultivation there and more work was underway at Bannockburn.[10]

By 1878 Fowler had supplied the Duke with 16 ploughing engines (8 pairs) ranging in size from 6 to 16 nominal horsepower. These were complemented by 13 general purpose traction engines. The ploughing engines were used for clearing the soil of stone and roots, collecting the material brought to the surface, then preparing the ground in preparation for sowing. Special implements were developed for the reclamation work, including the massive Sutherland plough (designed by the Duke) with an attachment for stirring the subsoil, a sledge-mounted scoop for stones, a disc harrow (designed by George Grieg, noted previously in his connection with the Kincardineshire Steam Ploughing Company) and a cart for bringing water to the engines over rough ground. Where the implements could not dislodge the buried roots, dynamite was employed. Steam engines were also used to pull groups of live trees, roots and all, from the soil. Not surprisingly given its heavy use, the machinery occasionally broke down, and workshops were established at Brora for carrying out repairs and maintenance.[11]

There was great interest in the Sutherland reclamations whilst they were being carried out, and the works were reported in detail in the popular and technical press. The use of steam power particularly elicited positive comment:

As an example of the rough and heavy work which can be performed by modern steam ploughing tackle, the operations in Sutherlandshire possess great interest, and they prove that such tackle is susceptible of many applications differing materially from those to which it is ordinarily devoted. To Messrs. Fowler and Co. great credit is due for the manner in which they have developed such machinery, and for showing how it is possible by the employment of good designs combined with first class materials and workmanship, to get engines to satisfactorily stand an amount of rough usage quite unthought of in the earlier days of steam cultivation.[12]

The technology may have worked at one level, but modern understanding of the ecology of delicate habitats like moss and moorland shows that disturbing the soil structure in this way does more harm than good.

Ultimately the scheme was neither a financial nor agricultural success. Its completion coincided with the onset of an agricultural depression, and by 1883 the enormous outlay of £210,000 had generated an increase in rent of only £200 per annum. Ten years later less than a quarter of the reclaimed land was still being farmed, and relations between the Sutherland tenantry and the estate had moved from optimism to disappointment.[13]

STEAM AND DYNAMITE

FOWLER SINGLE-CYLINDER
PLOUGHING ENGINE WITH
SUTHERLAND PLOUGH,
LOCH SHIN, 1874

(© National Museums Scotland)

As with conventional steam cultivation, two engines were used, each hauling the Sutherland plough to and fro. A contemporary account states that

> … the plough turned over a furrow about 2 feet deep, and that the 'Duke's toothpick', or the anchor-like hook that followed the plough, loosened the subsoil without throwing it over the furrow. The large stones were taken out by men who followed the plough; and, when large tree-roots were met with, the wire-rope was detached from the plough and fixed on these roots, and thus they were torn from their mossy beds with marvellous despatch. In this operation extraordinary masses of earth were sometimes moved.

> In cases where it was found more convenient, dynamite was used in dislodging these roots, which were very numerous in some parts; and they were hauled by steam to the edge of the field or section on a huge platform, shaped like a sledge, about 24 feet long by 12 feet wide. When dry and cut up they made excellent fuel for the engines, and were largely used for that purpose.[14]

Dislodged rocks and roots are visible in the foreground, and a pile of cut roots is shown stacked beside the engine, ready for feeding into the firebox.

Engineering, 10 December 1875, p. 453

Above:

SUTHERLAND PLOUGH WITH 'DUKE'S TOOTHPICK', 1874

Three of these ploughs, designed expressly for use on the Sutherland reclamations, were made at John Fowler's Steam Plough Works in Leeds. They were pulled by a 16 nominal horsepower engine, geared to work at half the usual ploughing speed. When used at Kildonan the plough was adapted to mix the surface and subsoil '*by attaching a huge mouldboard to what is known as the "Duke's toothpick," or the anchor-shaped subsoiler which follows in the furrow behind the main plough. This new application brought a very large additional strain on the engine, and during the summer of 1877 frequent consequent breakage hindered the progress of the work, and also tended to increase the expense.*'[15]

The Engineer, 24 July 1874, p. 82

(© Both images: National Museums Scotland)

Below: FOWLER SINGLE-CYLINDER PLOUGHING ENGINE WITH STONE SCOOP, 1874

The stones extracted by the Sutherland plough are employed in the construction of roads, walls, buildings, &c., and to collect them a kind of sledge is employed. … This sledge is hauled to any desired point by one of the engines, and is then tipped by the opposite engine hauling on the tail rope.[16]

With the ground cleared, conventional steam-cultivating implements could then be used. The canvas sheet used to cover the cylinder and motion of the ploughing engine when not working is draped on the roof, and the end of the rod with attached brush for sweeping out the boiler tubes is just visible above the further front wheel.

Engineering, 10 December 1875, p. 452

Threshing

One of the most laborious tasks on the farm was separating the grain from the previously reaped sheaves of oats, wheat or barley. Andrew Meikle from East Lothian developed the first successful machine for this in 1786, and by the early 1800s his invention had spread throughout Scotland and into England. From this time a winnower to separate the grain from the chaff was often incorporated into the machine, the whole being fixed into the farm steading. The first examples were powered by water, horse or wind, and from the 1830s larger lowland farms installed stationary steam engines for this purpose. In the twentieth century these were replaced by oil engines.[17]

Portable threshing machines, pioneered in England by Ransomes of Ipswich in the 1840s, began to spread throughout Scotland from the late 1850s. Mounted on strong wheels, they were able to be moved from farm to farm, and so in Scotland were called travelling mills. By the 1870s these mills were often fitted with apparatus to clean and grade the threshed grain.[18] This made them heavier, and whilst the first travelling mills could be pulled by horse (and driven by a horse-drawn portable steam engine), later machines were usually hauled and powered by an agricultural, or general purpose, traction engine.

For some time in Scotland the two systems of threshing co-existed. The fixed mill in the steading allowed farmers to thresh grain and make fresh straw for animal feed and bedding as it was needed. The high-capacity travelling mill augmented this, and allowed large quantities of grain grown as a cash crop to be expeditiously prepared for sale at market, to feed the growing urban population. Ultimately the combine harvester, introduced into East Lothian in 1932 and widespread by the 1960s, made redundant the previously separate tasks of reaping, binding, stooking, stacking and finally threshing the crop.[19]

The travelling threshing mill demanded large numbers of people for its operation. An account of best practice in Ayrshire in 1879 recommended that no less than seven men, four women and two boys were needed, not including the 'engineers' (the engine driver and his mate, who took it in turns to feed the sheaves into the threshing mill):

> One man will fork the sheaves on to the feeding platform, two women will loose them, three men with the assistance of a boy to hold the straps (already made) will bunch, tie and dress the sheaves [of threshed straw] handsomely, one woman will convey them to the forker, who in turn will pass them to the builder [of the straw stack], one woman to remove the chaff to its destination, one man with the aid of a barrow will bag, weigh, tie and deposit the wheat in any suitable house forty yards distant from the mill, and one boy to attend the engine with water.

Four of these people were dedicated to bundling up the threshed straw, in addition to the work carried out beforehand of preparing hundreds of oat straw straps five feet long for tying it.[20] In 1883 the trusser was developed by Howard of Bedford to perform this laborious task,[21] and surviving contemporary photographs indicate that a number of travelling threshing mills in Scotland were equipped with one, either attached to the mill or wheeled up to it. Where a trusser was not used, the straw was usually passed onto a long folding elevator and built into a large stack, or a baler might be located behind the mill and powered from it, making rectangular high density bales of straw. A chaff-cutter could be powered from the engine simultaneously with the threshing mill,[22] but this was not often seen as chaff-cutting was usually carried out on a dedicated machine in the farm steading. The typical travelling mill had a threshing drum 54 inches wide, and was powered by a traction engine of six or seven nominal horsepower. Such a mill could process around 700 bushels of grain per ten-hour day.[23]

Judging from the photographic record, the travelling threshing mills used in Scotland were usually made by one or other of the English firms who also made the associated traction engines, including Marshalls of Gainsborough and Ransomes of Ipswich. The engine and its mill were not necessarily made by the same firm, as some users favoured differing makes of each. (It should be noted that although Fowler made many traction engines, they did not make threshing mills.) Garvie of Aberdeen, Allan Brothers of Aberdeen, and Crighton of Turriff made some travelling mills too, but concentrated largely on supplying the market for stationary threshing mills installed in Scottish steadings.

THRESHING

Above:

MID 19TH-CENTURY STEAM THRESHING COMPLEX, WATERSTONE FARM, WEST LOTHIAN

Before the advent of the travelling mill, threshing was carried out by stationary mills that were fixed into a building. Here the boiler and steam engine to power the threshing mill was housed in the smaller central building, with the chimney from the boiler rising from its far end. Coal for fuel was readily available from the many mines located in the Lothians. The mill was located in the tall building on the left. This photograph was taken by John R. Hume.

(© Royal Commission on the Ancient and Historical Monuments of Scotland, Licensor www.scran.ac.uk)

Below:

THRESHING AT BRIDGEHEUGH, SELKIRK, *c.*1920

A Ruston-Hornsby compound traction engine is hard at work driving a Ransomes, Sims & Jefferies threshing mill with a Hornsby straw trusser attached. The man in the centre is forking a sheaf up to the feeder on top of the mill, and there are four more stacks behind the mill still to be threshed.

(© Robert D. Clapperton Photographic Trust, Licensor www.scran.ac.uk)

TRAVELLING MILL THRESHING IN EDZELL AREA, ANGUS, c.1910

A long belt (made from leather or canvas) is taking power from the McLaren single-cylinder traction engine to the mill made by Clayton & Shuttleworth of Lincoln.

A long elevator behind the mill is being used to stack the threshed straw and a water cart with its large barrel is providing water for the engine.

(© National Museums Scotland, Scottish Life Archive)

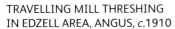

PRICE LIST OF PORTABLE THRASHING MACHINES, c.1935

These portable thrashing machines were made by Allan Brothers, Aberdeen, c.1935. Each was supplied with a waterproof cover and a screw jack, essential for lifting the machine so that it could be chocked perfectly horizontal (both length- and cross-wise) in order to separate the grain and straw properly. Pneumatic tyres are fitted, allowing the machine to be hauled between jobs at a higher road speed than when fitted with iron or wooden wheels.

(© National Museums Scotland, SLA W.MS.1980.50.2)

THRESHING

Right: JAMES SMITH'S McLAREN TRACTION ENGINE AND CLAYTON & SHUTTLEWORTH MILL, PERTH, 1910

A wheeled trusser has been placed against the end of the mill and the barn doors are open, ready for the trussed straw. The engine has been fixed in position to keep the long drive belt tensioned; there is a chock in front of the rear wheel, which is held against the chock by a screw jack.

(© National Museums Scotland)

Below: THRESHING NEAR WICK, *c.*1910

Messrs Allan's Fowler single-cylinder traction engine driving a threshing machine and elevator (possibly made by Robey of Lincoln). The stacks of grain (probably oats) have been threshed simultaneously and are nearly finished; the folded tarpaulin on top of the mill will be used to cover it over as soon as work is done.

(© Photograph reproduced courtesy of Caithness Horizons Collections Trust)

76

Haulage

Road steamers

As agricultural and industrial output grew during the nineteenth century, the traction engine found increasing use in moving loads of all kinds by road. In chapter 1 we saw one of Alexander Chaplin's large traction engines being used in 1866 for haulage in Glasgow, and by the early 1870s a fleet of road steamers to R. W. Thomson's design were being employed by F. C. de Lousada, providing the only practical alternative then available to teams of horses, or even hundreds of men, for moving heavy components from Glasgow foundries and engineering works to the docks.

> *Formerly it was the practice to employ horses alone for hauling these articles; but it was practically impossible to get all the horses to pull together when the weight became considerable, say 20 tons or more, and hence there was a great loss of power. By-and-by it was found to be more satisfactory to have the hauling done by large bodies of workmen, especially when the weights amounted to 20 tons or upwards. Now, as this sort of traction work involved the employment of 8 or 10 men for every ton weight to be moved, it will at once be seen that the hauling of a boiler of say, 40 tons, would call into requisition the services of probably not fewer than 400 workmen, operating in rows through four or five ropes or even more. … Most of the men would be skilled mechanics, and during that time, therefore, the productive power of the boiler works, engine works, &c., would be suspended; and on that account alone the operation would be a very expensive one, in addition to being one of great inconvenience to the public.*

In 1874 de Lousada's company had four road steamers (made by Tennant in Leith): three of 12-horsepower and one of 8-horsepower. Another haulage company, J. C. Brown, had a further three road steamers at work.[24] Typical of the restrictions generally imposed on hauliers by road and bridge authorities across Scotland, the Glasgow operators had to cope with weight limits on road bridges over the River Clyde, and restrictions on daylight working in the city centre. Some of the road steamers remained in use into the 1930s, supplemented by more modern haulage engines.[25]

HAULING

Road Steamers

Below:

FOUR THOMSON ROAD STEAMERS, GLASGOW, *c.*1875

Two large new Scotch marine boilers, ready for craning into a steamship, are positioned on the quayside at Mavisbank by two pairs of road steamers. The larger are 12-horsepower; the smaller engine at the front of the load is 8-horsepower.

(John R. Hume Collection)

Above:

TWO 12-HORSEPOWER ROAD STEAMERS, *c.*1920

These road steamers are hauling a marine boiler. The dented water tank testifies to half a century of hard work around Glasgow's docks. Note the linked steel plates protecting the face of the rubber tyres on the rear wheels.

(© National Museums Scotland)

Country Haulage

Much road haulage was performed by general purpose traction engines too, especially in rural areas where the engines could also be used to power agricultural machinery. In some cases the availability of steam haulage influenced patterns of cultivation, for instance in the north-east of Scotland in the 1880s. Here potatoes were able to be grown further from the railhead or ports as increasingly numerous traction engines, capable of travelling longer distances and hauling bigger loads, provided an economic alternative to horse-drawn carts.[26] Sometimes ordinary four-wheel farm wagons would be hitched behind the engine to carry the load, but many traction engine makers also supplied heavily-built wagons (described as traction wagons) more suited to steam haulage.

McLAREN SINGLE-CYLINDER GENERAL PURPOSE TRACTION ENGINE, *c.*1910

This engine, owned by John Turnbull, is hauling two traction wagons loaded with sacks of threshed grain at Chirnside. The third man leaning against the engine walked alongside and controlled the brakes on the two wagons. If horses were encountered on the road, everything came to a halt and the third man would be on hand to lead them past.

(© National Museums Scotland, SLA C25691)

HAULING

Country Haulage

Above:

MARSHALL SINGLE-CYLINDER TRACTION ENGINE

Marshall single-cylinder traction engine belonging to Messrs Gunn ready to set off with two well-laden wagons of furniture and other effects, Thurso, *c.*1910. A hurricane paraffin lamp is hanging from the tray on the front axle to provide a little illumination after dark.

(© Photograph reproduced courtesy of Caithness Horizons Collections Trust)

Below:

AVELING & PORTER TRACTION ENGINE

Aveling & Porter traction engine no. 1988 of 1884 hauling timber at Elcho Castle, Perthshire in 1917. The engine and trailer belonged to James Halliday (standing on the left), a local timber merchant. The driver is David Gannon and the steersman is Robert Sharp. The trunk of the giant oak tree contained 240 cubic feet of timber and weighed 11 tons.

(© National Museums Scotland, SLA C2871)

Road Locomotives

From the 1880s some English makers offered a version of traction engine specially adapted for heavy haulage. These were described as road locomotives, and constructed on a more substantial scale than their equivalent size of general purpose traction engine. They had spring suspension on their front and rear axles for rough roads, and carried extra water for the boiler so that they could travel for longer without having to stop and refill their tanks. Compound cylinders for economy in fuel and water were usually fitted; this was an important consideration for the operator when he had to supply both. Some road locomotives were fitted with three speeds rather than the two commonly found on general purpose traction engines, allowing them to travel faster. The engine and flywheel spokes were covered, ostensibly to prevent any horses encountered on the road being frightened by the flashing of moving parts. Some road locomotives were fitted with a large crane, which was useful when loading or installing cumbersome items like stationary boilers and engines. The jib was mounted on a bracket at the front of the engine, and the winding hoist driven from the engine crankshaft. One such crane engine – an 8-horsepower road locomotive made by Fowler in 1901 – was used by an engineering firm in Leith.

T. C. Kerr of Mavisbank built up a fleet of road locomotives from 1899, mainly using engines made by Burrell of Thetford. His company was based on the south side of the Clyde (opposite the Road Steam Engine Company operating Thomson road steamers on the north side) and worked throughout Scotland and into England. In 1912 Kerr took delivery of a new road locomotive named 'Clyde'. This was the largest road engine made for the British market by Burrell, and with it Kerr was able to go into competition with the Road Steam Engine Company for the haulage of very heavy loads. A special trailer, nicknamed the 'Loch Ness Monster', was constructed in 1926 to carry massive loads of up to 150 tons. In 1932 the two firms amalgamated to form Road Engines & Kerr (Haulage) Limited. The ancient road steamers were scrapped and a consolidated fleet incorporating one Fowler, two Burrell, and three McLaren road locomotives carried on, tackling amongst other jobs the near-heroic move of large electrical equipment for Scottish hydro-electric schemes in remote parts of the Highlands. Some of these transformers appeared very much to have come from a different technological era from the road locomotives, whose final tasks in the 1940s returned them to their origins, moving boilers, ship components, and, perhaps best known of all, railway locomotives. Many were hauled from the North British Locomotive Company works in Springburn to Clydeside for craning on board ships for export. In 1948 Road Engines & Kerr was nationalised, and from this time diesel lorries and haulage tractors took over.[27]

HAULING

Road Locomotives

Above:

LANCASHIRE BOILER EN ROUTE TO ALLOA, c.1930

Two of Kerr's road locomotives (McLaren leading a Burrell) are pictured hauling a new Lancashire boiler, made by Penman of Glasgow, to Robert Younger's brewery at Alloa. No brakes were fitted to the bogies carrying the boiler, and the engines had to slow or stop the load. A trailer carrying coal for the engines is at the end of the train.

(John R. Hume Collection)

Below:

SETTING OFF FROM QUEEN'S PARK LOCOMOTIVE WORKS TO GLASGOW DOCKS, c.1930

Two Burrell road locomotives, 'Lord Roberts' and 'Clyde', are hauling a trailer carrying a railway locomotive being shipped to Egypt, watched by a good crowd. A third McLaren road locomotive (its roof just visible behind the trailer) was used to help with reversing the load, braking on the road, and then positioning the trailer under the crane at the docks.

(© National Museums Scotland, SLA 92P3A)

Showman's road locomotives

Special road locomotives were used by travelling showmen for towing fairground rides and attractions to events throughout Scotland linked to local hiring fairs and holidays. These machines were usually colourful and highly decorated, and carried a large dynamo, driven by the engine when stationary, to generate electricity for lighting and sometimes powering the rides. The years around the First World War saw the high point of steam-hauled, steam-powered fairs and the leading suppliers of engines to showmen at this time were Burrell and Fowler. Focussing on Burrell's output, John Evans of Portobello took delivery of a new six horse-power showman's road locomotive 'Edinburgh Castle' in 1904 and an 8- horsepower engine the following year. A. H. Faulkner of Leith acquired Burrell 'Perseverance Leith' in 1908, and in 1913 no less than five new Burrell road locomotives were supplied to Scottish showmen. One of these engines, 'Rajah', was made for E. H. Bostock of Glasgow, proprietor of the famous Bostock & Wombwell's travelling menagerie, and it was joined by a similar showman's road locomotive 'Nero' in 1915. Together they hauled the mobile zoo, packed into large wagons, to fairs throughout Scotland and England, becoming the furthest-travelled showman's road locomotives in Britain. In 1920 Burrell 'Queen Elizabeth' was delivered to J. Wilmot in Glasgow, equipped with a jib crane which could be attached to the rear of the engine and used to help build up and dismantle the large and complex rides which were then becoming fashionable on the fairground.[28]

HAULING

Steam on the Fairground

Above:

ROOD FAIR, DUMFRIES, *c.*1910

The large roundabouts and the switch-back ride in the centre of the photograph were transported between fairs, dismantled into pieces and loaded into wagons called 'packing trucks', which were hauled by showman's road locomotives.

(© Dumfries Museum, Licensor www.scran.ac.uk)

Below:

FOWLER SHOWMAN'S ROAD LOCOMOTIVE, *c.*1910

'Indomitable', Fowler no. 11440 of 1908, was owned by C. & J. Howard of Glasgow. The 'Twin Yachts' was an exciting ride (with its own steam engine) consisting of a pair of large swingboats which oscillated at speed. 'Indomitable' has delivered the ride to the fairground, and is now parked with a belt running from the flywheel to the dynamo, ready to generate electricity for lighting the ride.

(© Grampian Transport Museum, Aberdeen)

Left:

POSTER FOR BOSTOCK & WOMBWELL'S 'MONSTER COMBINED SHOW', LANARK, MAY 1919

(© South Lanarkshire Libraries and Community Learning, Licensor www.scran.ac.uk)

Below:

BOSTOCK & WOMBWELL'S MENAGERIE ON THE ROAD

Burrell showman's road locomotives 'Rajah' and 'Nero' coupled together on the road, c.1920. A living van is attached to the back of the road train, behind the two large wagons.

(© National Fairground Archive, University of Sheffield)

Steam on the Fairground

AVELING & PORTER
5-TON COMPOUND STEAM TRACTOR
AND WAGON

This Aveling steam tractor, registration SX458 and builder's number 8465 of 1915, was owned by Bathgate District Committee Roads Department in West Lothian.

The photograph was taken in a quarry in Bathgate, c.1920. The heavy wooden traction wagon is empty, ready for loading with stone for road making. It was also made by Aveling & Porter, and incorporated a mechanism for tipping the

body to unload its contents. The cover plates over the ends of the tractor's compound cylinders have been decorated with small brass stars, either by the driver or by staff at the council depot, indicating their pride in the machine. The driver stands by the front wheel, and the handle of the long rod for sweeping out the boiler tubes is by his left hand. The three boys are perhaps his children.

(© National Museums Scotland, SLA C1505)

Steam tractors

Smaller haulage engines were known as steam tractors. They proliferated in the early years of the twentieth century after legislation was passed permitting them to be driven at five miles per hour and by one man. This was instead of a driver and separate steersman, as continued to be required on larger machines.[29] In Scotland they were popular with local authorities for hauling road-making materials, or coal or coke from railway station to council yard. Early in 1905 Perthshire County Council conducted an experiment with 'Steam motor haulage' in place of horse haulage for carrying road metal. This allowed the stone to be brought direct from the quarry to the roadside, placing it ready for steam rolling. Following a four-month trial, the council's surveyor reported that steam haulage was 36 per cent cheaper (after making allowance for fuel, oil, cleaning materials and depreciation) than horse haulage.[30] By October 1907, Aveling & Porter of Rochester had supplied the following Scottish county councils with steam tractors: Peebles, Lanark, Stirling (two), Clackmannan and Ayr (two).[31]

Steam wagons

The legislative changes that gave rise to the steam tractor also resulted in a number of firms producing steam wagons from the early 1900s. In addition to Sentinel and the other Scottish makes examined in chapter 1, significant numbers of wagons were made in England by

Aveling & Porter, Garrett of Leiston in Suffolk, and Foden of Sandbach in Cheshire, amongst others. They could carry a range of bodies: flat bed for bulky loads like sacks, barrels and timber; tanks for liquids; or hinged sides (sometimes tipping) to hold stone, coal or other minerals. Early wagons had no weather protection for the driver, but later machines had enclosed cabs and even windscreens like a motor lorry. Compact and fast, they were popular in Scotland with hauliers, merchants (the Scottish Co-operative Wholesale Society in Glasgow bought seven new Sentinels between 1908 and 1910[32]) and distillers. The early wagons could carry around three tons, with larger and later wagons able to carry up to 13 tons. When fitted with pneumatic tyres in the 1930s, some Sentinel steam wagons were able to travel at speeds of 30 miles per hour or more. The faster, newer machines remained in use until well after the end of the Second World War.

Above:

SENTINEL STEAM WAGON

Sentinel steam wagon, owned by the Great North of Scotland Railway, being loaded with sacks of flour in Aberdeen Harbour, c.1907. This early wagon has no cab to shelter the driver from the weather. The Great North of Scotland Railway used three of these early Sentinels to provide a door-to-door service for the collection and delivery of rail freight, thus extending the reach of its operations in Aberdeenshire.

(© Grampian Transport Museum, Aberdeen)

Below:

FODEN STEAM WAGON 'BUSY BEE'

Foden steam wagon no. 3564 of 1913, registration M4726, and trailer loaded with logs, in Glamis Road, Dundee, 1926. Like many such machines it had a number of owners over the course of its working life. It was first used by A. Craik in Alyth for carting stone. In 1923 it was sold to John Doe, a haulage contractor in Errol. The wheels on the wagon and trailer are fitted with solid rubber tyres, which together with the simple spring suspension fitted, alleviated the worst of the shocks and bumps caused by the roads of the time.

(© National Museums Scotland, SLA C2975)

HAULAGE

Steam Wagons

Above:

SENTINEL STANDARD WAGON

Sentinel Standard 6-ton wagon, registration SA 5216 and builder's number 4040 of 1922, at Glendronach Distillery, Huntly. Two polished brass lamps with oil burners are fitted to each side of the driver's cab, and there is a larger single acetylene headlamp on the front apron.

Below (left): **GARRETT WAGON**

Garrett wagon no. 34241 of 1923, registration RS 5367, and trailer, owned by Town & County Motor Garages, Aberdeen. The load appears to be barrel staves, suggesting that the wagon is en route from a sawmill to a cooperage in a brewery, distillery or fish-packers.

Below (right):

SENTINEL DG6 WAGON

Sentinel DG6 wagon no. 7729 of 1929, registration GE 3897, carrying the livery of The Universal Transport Company (Scotland) Ltd, Glasgow. The DG6 was an improved model of Sentinel, introduced in 1927. The cab has a windscreen, and electric headlights are now fitted making night time journeys easier for the driver, although the side lamps still have oil burners like the earlier Standard Sentinel. From the gloss of the paintwork, this wagon appears to be new, or nearly so, and the designation 'Route 5' above the windscreen indicates that it was to be used on one of a number of scheduled routes operated by Universal Transport.

(© All images: Grampian Transport Museum, Aberdeen)

Road Rolling

Road making and mending

As the volume and the speed of road traffic increased through the nineteenth and twentieth centuries, the repair and construction of roads assumed ever greater importance across Scotland, with the steam roller becoming an essential tool for this. These machines were very similar to the general purpose traction engine, but with smooth rolls in place of the driving and front wheels. Like road locomotives, the engine and flywheel were covered over so as not to aggravate other horse traffic. As we have seen in chapter 1, there was a handful of Scottish-made steam rollers produced in the mid- to late nineteenth century, but like the traction engine, most Scottish needs were supplied by English firms. Two predominated: Aveling & Porter (by 1907 it had sold more than 130 steam rollers to Scottish county councils stretching from Caithness to Dumfriesshire, with more owned by town and city authorities[33]) and Fowler. Thus Scotland's direct contribution to good roads came more from the work of civil engineers Thomas Telford and John McAdam, rather than its very few steam roller makers. Wherever there were roads in Scotland, there was usually a steam roller not too far away – not only on the mainland but on Islay, Orkney and Shetland too.

Early roads were constructed from graded pieces of stone, carefully rolled into a cambered shape to drain off rainwater, following guidelines laid down by McAdam in 1825. The steam rollers used typically weighed 10–12 tons, although sometimes machines weighing up to 18 tons were used to compact the base in a newly constructed stretch of road. As traffic passed over these roads the surface stone broke up, causing the road to become muddy in wet weather and dusty in summer. The road then needed to be repaired, with potholes filled and new stone rolled on top. The experience of a road surveyor in rural Berwickshire following the winter of 1907–1908 was typical:

> *Following the slight frosts there was considerable lifting of the surface at places, and on one or two lines of road on which heavy traffic was thrown the surface was entirely broken through. …*
>
> *Traction engine, motor waggon [sic.] and motor car traffic appears to be steadily increasing in the district, and the bad effect of the traffic on the roads has become more apparent. The effect of the grip and suction of the tyres of motor cars, especially those travelling at high speed, is to remove the binding material of the metalling, which being thus exposed is more liable to be broken up or crushed by the iron-shod traffic.*
>
> *In order to counteract the damage done by the traffic referred to, and to maintain the roads in a reasonable state of repair, it will be necessary to increase the quantity of metal (i.e. road stone) very considerably.*[34]

Following demands for improved smooth and dust-less roads, tar was first used to bind the surface (sometimes sprayed from a steam wagon or even the roller itself), and later on bitumen mixtures were introduced. In a reference to McAdam's name, such surfaces became known as tarmacadam, or tarmac. For bitumen surfaces smaller steam (or sometimes motor) rollers were produced from the 1920s, which being lighter and a little faster did not sink into the soft asphalt (a mix of bitumen, sand and stone) as they were rolling it.[35] A large number of these were made by Fowler, who also continued to sell general purpose steam rollers to Scottish local authorities into the late 1930s.

Some steam rollers were produced which were able to be converted to a traction engine (or steam tractor if small), and vice versa, by making the front rolls and their supporting forecarriage interchangeable with a conventional two-wheeled front axle. The rear rolls would then be swapped for driving wheels better able to grip the road. This allowed the one machine to be used to haul stone from the quarry, and then, after much effort with lifting jacks and spanners, set to work rolling it. Sometimes such convertible engines were fitted with a governor so that they could also be used to power a stationary stone crusher. Whilst in theory this was an appealing idea in making capital plant work harder and longer, it is telling that most such machines ended their days permanently in road roller form, especially once cheaper motor lorries were available to take over haulage duties.

Above:

AVELING & PORTER 10-TON STEAM ROLLER, *c.*1900

An Aveling & Porter steam roller constructing a new surface on a section of the Perth to Inverness road (the present A9), Perthshire at the turn of the twentieth century. A horse and cart is delivering stone for spreading by the workmen before being rolled flat. The rims on the rolls are quite thick, suggesting that the steam roller is fairly new. The driver is David Robertson.

(© National Museums Scotland, SLA C5684)

Below:

LAYING DRAINS AT AUCHTERMUCHTY, FIFE, *c.*1930

Aveling & Porter 8-ton steam roller no. 12072 of 1928, owned by contractor Robert Terras. The roller has a scarifier attached to the side of the tender behind the rear roll. The scarifier had three or four sharp steel tines which could be lowered into the road surface to break it up. This made it easier to start to dig a trench (as here for drain pipes), or for potholed surfaces to be remade.

(© National Museums Scotland, SLA C2712)

ROAD MAKING AND MENDING

Above: THE CARE OF THE ROAD

Early issues of *The Motor World* magazine contained information to keep motorists up-to-date with road works around Scotland, for example 'ARGYLL-SHIRE ... Loch Fyne road, between Lochgair and Minard – Bottoming, coating and rolling operations. Road very narrow, and drivers should go slowly in passing ...'.[36] An Aveling & Porter steam roller and motor car feature in this heading for 'The care of the road' report in 1913.

(© National Museums Scotland, source, *The Motor World*, 23 January 1913, p.107)

Above: SENTINEL STANDARD STEAM WAGON

Sentinel Standard steam wagon, number 2487, registration AW 5333, at John o' Groats Hotel, *c*.1925. The wagon is owned by H. V. Smith; the wording 'Trinidad Asphalt Macadam' on the cab front indicates that Smith supplied naturally occurring asphalt imported from the island of Trinidad.

(© Scottish Motor Museum Trust, Licensor www.scran.ac.uk)

Right: FOWLER COMPOUND STEAM ROLLER

Fowler compound steam roller, number 16235, registration AV 45, in Aberdeenshire. This roller was new in May 1924, and was fitted with Woods's patent tar spraying equipment. The tar is stored in the heated rectangular tank beneath the boiler, with a pump driven by chain from the crankshaft. A hose for spraying tar by hand hangs from the tank, and there was also a sprayer bar extending the width of the roller fixed at the rear. In use the road would first be repaired, levelled and swept before the tar was sprayed on. Small stone chippings were then spread over the liquid tar, and then rolled in.

(© Grampian Transport Museum, Aberdeen)

ROAD MAKING AND MENDING

Above:

MARSHALL TRACTION ENGINE STONE CRUSHING IN FIFE

Marshall single-cylinder traction engine no. 73186 of 1920, registration SP 6081, driving a stone crushing and grading machine in a quarry in Fife. Stone is being delivered to the crusher by wheelbarrow, and the wheel of a horse cart for taking the crushed stone away can just be seen at the left of the photograph. The hose at the rear of the engine is attached to a water lifter inside the tender, and is used to draw water from a barrel or stream and deliver it into the engine's water tank.

(© Grampian Transport Museum, Aberdeen)

Below:

AVELING & PORTER COMPOUND STEAM ROLLER ON SHETLAND

Aveling & Porter compound steam roller no. 11158, registration PS558, resting at the roadside on Shetland. This 8-ton machine was registered to Zetland County Council on 27 April 1925. It is a convertible steam roller; the front roll could be detached by undoing the bolts on the front of the smokebox (beneath the number plate) and a traction engine axle then fitted beneath the smokebox. There is a small rectangular tank on the roof, which given the distance of coal supplies from Shetland may have stored fuel oil for firing the boiler in place of the usual coal. Another local adaptation is the extension to the chimney to improve the draft for the fire. The roller was scrapped at Girlsta in c.1950, and this photograph was probably taken shortly before this date.

(© Shetland Museum and Archives)

Contracting

We have seen the role of the steam cultivation companies of the 1860s and 1870s in making expensive machinery available to those Scottish farmers who could not, or did not, wish to invest the large sum required for its purchase. For the same reason businesses were established from this time for hiring high output threshing machinery which farmers would need to use only occasionally. Other contractors specialised in civil engineering works and maintained fleets of steam rollers and wagons, such as William Dobson in Edinburgh, although in this field many local authorities chose to operate their own plant for road making and mending as this was such a constant task. A few contractors were equipped for a wide range of tasks, such as A. Cochrane of Greenlaw, Berwickshire, who operated steam ploughing engines, threshing tackle, steam wagons and road rollers.

Agricultural work provided the main instance of contracting (as this practice was called) in Scotland, with travelling steam-powered threshing mills comprising the greatest part of this. Contractors supplied all the machinery necessary to undertake a task, and the specialist labour for operating it. In the case of steam ploughing, this comprised the drivers (two being required where double-engine tackle was used) and a ploughman to control the implement, with support provided by a mate and a boy. A wooden living van with beds and a cooking stove would accompany the tackle to provide accommodation for the crew if they were far from their home base. With threshing, the usual contractor's outfit consisted of traction engine, mill, a trusser or baler and a van for the crew if necessary. The contractor provided the engine driver and a mate responsible for operating the mill. A third person was also needed to accompany the outfit on the road whilst travelling between jobs, even after the legal requirement for someone to precede the engine on foot whilst travelling between jobs was repealed. The farmer provided all the other labour to bring the sheaves to feed the mill and take away grain and straw, and the fuel and water for the engine.[37] Because of this last point, agricultural contractors seemed less concerned about economy in working their engines, tending to favour the simple single-cylinder machine over the compound engine which was more efficient, but also more complicated and costly to buy new.

Agricultural contractors ranged in size from the farmer with his own engine and equipment which he would hire to neighbours, up to large concerns with more than a dozen machines. Some rural contractors carried out steam cultivation as well as threshing, and haulage in between times. A good example of a contractor operating at the smaller end of the scale, and typical of many throughout the arable counties of Scotland, is John Turnbull from Chirnside in Berwickshire.

In 1889 Turnbull appears to have been based in nearby Kelso, and there purchased a pair of Fowler steam ploughing engines and plough, cultivator and harrows, together with a Marshall threshing mill and a straw elevator from J. & H. McLaren in Leeds. By 1894 he was located in Chirnside, and over the following nine

94

years bought five new 8-horsepower general purpose McLaren traction engines (all with single cylinders), part-exchanging a set of double-engine ploughing tackle against the price of the second traction engine in 1895. In 1914 a new road locomotive was purchased from John Fowler in Leeds.[38]

The growing number of new traction engines signalled threshing becoming the major part of Turnbull's work, and by the early 1900s mention of steam ploughing is dropped from the firm's billhead. Beside threshing, other jobs included sawing wood – either for firewood or planks – together with haulage of grain, lime, potatoes and road stone, and 'flitting' (removing house contents). Most of the threshing was carried out using a trusser to bundle up the straw delivered from the mill, for which Turnbull charged £2 and 5 shillings per day in 1909, whilst threshing only was charged at £1 and 15 shillings per day. The use of the trusser thus added nearly a third to the cost of threshing, and indicates how much more the bundled straw was valued because of its ease of handling.

John Turnbull died in 1912 and his widow took over the business, assisted by their older children. Trading continued until 1919, and from the list of lots at the closing sale we learn that the firm's assets at this time included three threshing sets (engine, mill and separate trusser), four wagons for towing by the traction engines (one of five tons capacity, the remainder able to carry eight tons) and a living van. With this equipment, the firm was able to serve communities in an approximate ten-mile radius from its base at the western end of Chirnside village, covering much of the eastern expanse of the Merse.[39]

The Turnbull sale may have been the delayed result of the death of John Turnbull, but in the same year A. Cochrane & Company also auctioned much of its varied plant. Both sales were conducted by Shirlaw Allan & Company of Hamilton, who specialised in this market. The advertised reason for Cochrane's sale was that the company was 'adopting Motor Haulage'.[40] Following the end of the First World War, hundreds of war-surplus lorries became available at low prices, encouraging many to move from steam to motor haulage.

In contrast, Raines of Stirling, a very large agricultural contracting business, concentrated on threshing. This firm dated back to Thomas Raines of Stirling who owned eighteen Clayton & Shuttleworth 8-horsepower single-cylinder traction engines between 1874 and 1884. By the early twentieth century, the firm was constituted as a limited liability company, and on 1 February 1921 registered no less than 19 traction engines (of a variety of English makes) with the local authority as required by the Roads Act of 1920. A further two engines were added later to their fleet, and all were paired with threshing mills and baling presses working across Stirlingshire and west Fife. Of these, 17 were single-cylinder engines, with only four being compounds. The company kept threshing until August 1945 when a 'Highly Important Three Days' Sale of Threshing and Baling Plant' was held. By this time many of the engines were elderly, coal was expensive and new paraffin-fuelled tractors were becoming more readily available. Sixteen complete

CONTRACTING

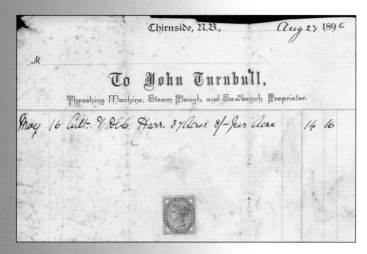

INVOICE, JOHN TURNBULL, 1896

Invoice issued by John Turnbull for cultivating and double-harrowing 37 acres of land on 16 May 1896. The billhead describes Turnbull as a 'Thrashing machine, steam plough, and sawbench proprietor'.

(© National Museums Scotland, W.MS.1996.19.13)

MEMORANDUM, JOHN TURNBULL, c.1900

Steam ploughing no longer appears on Turnbull's billhead, and has been replaced by steam haulage. The engraved illustration is of a McLaren single-cylinder traction engine of the type owned by Turnbull from 1895 onwards, and the printing block for this may have been lent by McLaren themselves.

(© National Museums Scotland, W.MS.1996.19.1)

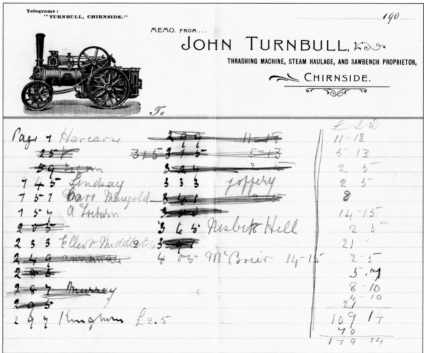

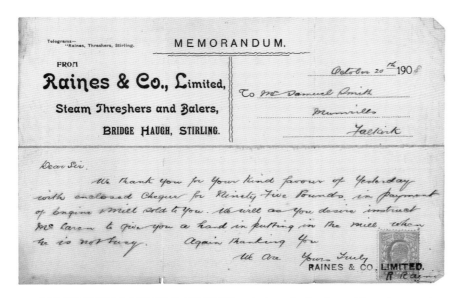

MEMORANDUM, RAINES & COMPANY LIMITED, 20 October 1908

The billhead describes the company as 'Steam threshers and balers', although in this instance the firm is supplying a steam engine and threshing mill to Samuel Smith of Falkirk.

(© National Museums Scotland, W.MS.1997.507.2)

threshing sets (traction engine and accompanying mill) were sold, with the engines fetching only scrap prices (averaging £36), whilst the threshing machines fetched much higher prices (average £640) because they were still useful and could be easily powered by tractor.[41]

Living and working with steam

Working with steam was demanding, whether driving the engine or attending the machinery it was ceaselessly powering. For the driver the day began early, waking to raise steam so that everything was ready when the morning shift began. The following excerpt comes from Cecil Mowbray, the driver of a council-owned 1925 Fowler steam roller based at Blairgowrie in the 1950s and 1960s, but the same basic tasks needed to be carried out whatever the engine:

My working day started about 5.30 a.m.. I'd get down to the yard by 6 a.m., unsheet the roller, check that the boiler was filled to the correct level and that all the fittings were in working order. Next the soot and dust from the smokebox and tubes was swept out to give a clear passage to the gases. Any clinker in the firebox grate had to be taken out together with the ash from the ashpan. The fire could then be lit, and while the water started to heat, I oiled all the motion work, filled the lubricators and grease caps on the engine and cleaned all the paint and brasswork. If you were lucky the firebox may have been banked up overnight, and then I just had to clear out the clinker. When all these jobs were done, I would nip home for breakfast while steam was being raised. By 7.30 a.m. I was on the road.

Cleaning out the tubes and steel chimney was the worst job. You had to rake them with long wire brushes, and when you were finished you were

AVELING & PORTER TRACTION ENGINE ACCIDENT AT KELSO, c.1901

Roxburghshire County Council's Aveling & Porter convertible traction engine number 3715 of 1896. The engine had just left the council depot in Kelso with two wagons loaded with road metal and got out of control descending Maxwellheugh Terrace. It ran across Jedburgh Road and then crashed into the wall of Cummings Temperance Hotel, fortunately without any injuries occurring.

(© Scottish Borders Council Museum & Gallery Service)

filthy black and covered in grease and grime. It had to be done every day because the efficiency of the roller depended on it. It was your roller and you maintained it. Once a year an inspector came along in a spotless white boiler suit and peered and poked about and went away still spotless. It made you think even more of all the hours spent on cleaning out the muck.[42]

Sometimes there were accidents. In 1872 the boiler on John Yule's large steam wagon exploded in Glasgow, killing ten people and injuring 50 others.[43] This was a catastrophic event, and gradually standards of boiler construction, maintenance and inspection improved. Some users, however, remained complacent about boiler safety. In 1894 an uninsured traction engine boiler exploded on the road between Peterhead and Aberdeen, severely scalding the driver and his assistant. The subsequent Board of Trade enquiry found that defects with the boiler and its fittings had not been sufficiently heeded by the owner. If the boiler had been inspected regularly by a surveyor from an insurance company, the faults would have been identified and required to be fixed in order for the boiler to continue to be insured.[44]

A more frequent occurrence was a traction engine with a heavy load getting out of control whilst descending a hill, and this was compounded when the roads were wet or icy. In extreme cases, on a long descent, the driver and steersman might jump from the engine to try and save their lives. There were also serious injuries associated with the operation of traction engines or the machinery being driven. Before the introduction of the guards and protective devices required by modern Health and Safely legislation, fast moving driving belts and exposed mechanisms could trap the hands and limbs of the tired, or careless, or unaware. In 1908 a driver from Cockburnspath was hurt badly when he fell from his engine and a pinion which he had been trying to fit on the crankshaft landed on his face.[45]

Left: ANGUS COUNCIL'S FOWLER ROLLER, KIRRIEMUIR DEPOT, 1966

Angus Council's Fowler roller no. 18295 of 1930, registration SR 7512 (later preserved as 'King o' the road'), in the Kirriemuir depot, September 1966. The ashpan has been removed and propped against the rear roll to allow access to the firebox for cleaning and inspection, and the door from the large manhole in the side of the boiler barrel has been removed. Some white asbestos oval gaskets are hanging on the wall above the workbench ready for fitting onto the man-hole door and the smaller doors covering the openings into the water space in the boiler. These openings allow mud and scale to be removed from the boiler, and for the inspector to see inside it.

(© RCAHMS. Reproduced courtesy of J. R. Hume. Licensor www.rcahms.gov.uk)

Right: MARSHALL GENERAL PURPOSE TRACTION ENGINE, ERROL

A Marshall general purpose traction engine at a blacksmith in Errol, Perthshire, 1925. The blacksmith Hector Reid stands by the rear wheel, holding the shaft of a heavy hammer which symbolised his trade. Blacksmiths were skilled at making or repairing items in wrought iron or mild steel, such as the hooks and haulage chains hanging from the tender at the rear of the traction engine.

(© National Museums Scotland, SLA C2973)

CARE AND MAINTENANCE

The driver was expected to undertake simple repairs and maintenance by the roadside or in the field, with larger and routine jobs undertaken back at the yard. Where spare parts were not obtained direct from the engine maker, the more elaborate repairs or components could be made by the local blacksmith or engineering works.

Below:

INVOICE, BINNEY & SON LIMITED, GLASGOW (21 February 1917)

Invoice from Binney & Son, Glasgow, including the supply of ten 'gauge glasses' (glass tubes for the water level gauges on a traction engine boiler).

(© National Museums Scotland W.MS.1996.19.36)

Below: INVOICE, ALEXANDER WAITE, CHIRNSIDE (30 May 1913)

Invoice to Mrs John Turnbull for traction engine parts and repairs. The invoice is from Alexander Wait, blacksmith in Chirnside, and includes repairs to a governor rod and a steering shaft, and making spud bolts (for attaching removable paddles to the rear wheels of a traction engine to give grip on soft or muddy ground).

(© National Museums Scotland, SLA C2373)

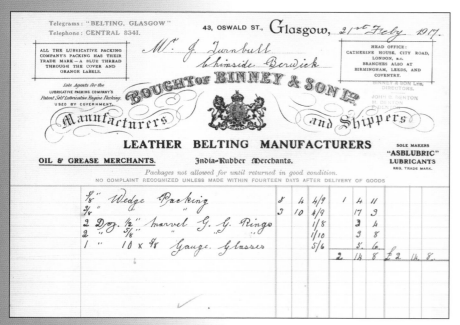

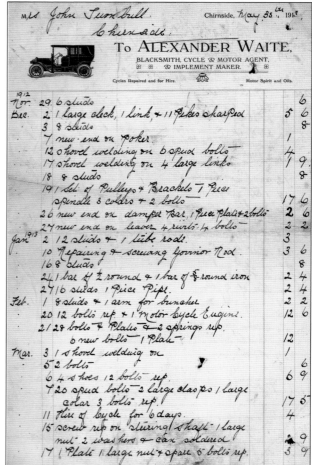

In 1893 the National Traction Engine Owners and Users Association was established in England. It provided insurance services and legal advice, and advocacy (like modern motoring organisations) to those in parliament and local authorities who were antagonistic to road steam locomotion. By 1907 a Scottish Traction Engine Owners and Users Association was well established, and that year held its Annual General Meeting at the Highland Show in Edinburgh. The president was Richard Raines, proprietor of Raines & Company of Stirling. A key preoccupation of the Scottish Association was the fact that owners in Scotland were still legally required to have a third man walking in front of a traction engine whilst on the move, warning other road users, even though this was no longer required in England. Their lobbying was successful, and this requirement was abolished by 1909. It would appear that local chapters of the Association were also formed, such as the Borders Traction Engine Owners and Users Association. In 1920 the National Association amalgamated with the National Threshing Machine Owners Association. Amongst other roles, it then set the prices to be charged by contractor members for threshing throughout the corn-growing regions of Britain, including Scotland.[46]

The most celebrated social interaction around the traction engine in Scotland arose from its use to power the travelling threshing mill.[47] Then even those whose encounter with steam would only be incidental, the farm workers, had reason to remember it. When threshing came around they had an arduous time, the mill seeming

to have an insatiable appetite for sheaves of corn and needing constant attendance to carry away the grain, chaff and straw. Help would be drafted in from nearby farms, and news and gossip would be exchanged. At the end of the long day there was something for all to look forward to, as recorded in Robert McEwen's account of threshing near Stirling around the mid-twentieth century:

Threshings were almost a social occasion, when neighbours would meet up and work together to help each other with the task. This was a handy set up as everybody could have a good squad of men who all knew what they were doing. Years later, after I left the school, we used to go to Archie McGibbon's threshings, which were the most memorable. … When the threshing day was finished, he and his sisters would entertain everyone with a slap up meal and a dram, a custom Archie had carried over from earlier generations.[48]

SENTINEL DG6 STEAM WAGON IN 1963

Sentinel DG6 steam wagon no. 8351 of 1930, registration RG1417, loading its hopper with cement whilst working on the Aberdeen south breakwater in May 1963.

(© Grampian Transport Museum, Aberdeen)

The end of the road

The end of steam power came at different times, and there was no one pattern to the life stories of traction engines in Scotland. As we have seen, these machines were, in general, heavily constructed and durable, which led to them often having working lives of several decades (or even longer) before they wore out and were scrapped. Sometimes they had shorter lives if worked very hard with poor maintenance, or were prototypes that were simply not up to the task. Occasionally engines were

adapted for a new role, or found a new use. The engineering firm of John M. Henderson & Company in Aberdeen constructed a mobile cable windlass on an old Fowler ploughing engine in 1894.[49] It was probably used in the construction of aerial cableways and bridges which were some of Henderson's key products. Similarly, a well-used Fowler ploughing engine appears on Victoria Pier in Lerwick in the 1890s, far from a likely landscape for steam cultivation.[50] It was presumably used there for haulage or driving machinery from its flywheel. Given their location, both of these engines may have begun their lives with one of the steam cultivating companies in the north of Scotland, or on the Sutherland land reclamations.

Because of its simple and robust nature, there were some instances of steam technology surviving well into the middle of the twentieth century, and even into the 1960s, by which time it was admittedly quite anachronistic. Key examples of this include the Sentinel steam wagon used by Cowlairs Co-operative Society for domestic coal deliveries in Springburn, and the Sentinels used in Aberdeen for harbour maintenance. Aberdeenshire, Angus and Perth councils all kept some of their newer steam rollers operating, and the last working general purpose traction engine, by Ransomes of Ipswich, winched coal from a private mine near Slamannan. These show how steam could still be an appropriate technology in particular circumstances. Where machinery was in serviceable condition (often because, dating from the 1920s or 1930s, it had not yet worn out), operating infrastructure was in place and skilled drivers available, and fuel was free or cheap, there was little sense in replacing it. Indeed, there are stories that some authorities kept on with steam because an older driver did not want to drive a modern diesel-powered machine. Certainly there was great affection for steam amongst the expert brotherhood that had grown up with it and mastered its intricacies. Cecil Mowbray, comparing his steam roller with a brand new diesel roller felt that 'Diesels have no heart or soul, it's just a wheel and a throttle and there's nothing else to do'.[51]

References

1. W. Fletcher, *The history and development of steam locomotion on common roads* (1891), pp. 259–276. Fletcher states that he is describing the ideal 'road locomotive', but he is in fact using the term in its legal sense (a steam-powered road vehicle) and the text describes the standard traction engine.
2. Highland and Agricultural Society of Scotland, Report on the present state of the agriculture of Scotland (1878), p. 149.
3. I. Carter, *Farmlife in northeast Scotland* (1979), p. 88; M. R. Lane, *The story of the Steam Plough Works: Fowlers of Leeds* (1980), pp. 16, 96–97.
4. The figures for steam cultivation are drawn from J. Macdonald, *Stephens' book of the farm* (1908), vol. 1, p. 423; those for horse ploughing were supplied by Elaine Edwards, National Museum of Rural Life Scotland (email to the author, 26 November 2010).
5. *Engineering*, 10 February 1871, p. 112; 16 June 1871, p. 423 (quote from p. 112).
6. J. Cruikshank, *Changes in the agricultural industry of Aberdeenshire in the last fifty years* (1935), pp. 4–5; Carter (1979), op. cit. (note 3), pp. 89–90, 203 (ref. 64).
7. Anon., 'The late Mr Andrew Gilchrist, J. P., Carvenom', Extract from East of Fife Record,

24 August 1911 [National Museums Scotland W.MS.1985.52.2].
8. *The Engineer*, 21 June 1918, pp. 527–28; J. Brown, *Steam on the farm: a history of agricultural steam engines 1800–1950* (2008), p. 129. The 10-horsepower engine is Fowler no. 15405; the larger pair are Fowler nos 15451 and 15452: J. B. True and B. Johnson, *The traction engine register* (2008), pp. 41–42.
9. J. McDonald, 'On the agriculture of the county of Sutherland', *Transactions of the Highland and Agricultural Society of Scotland*, 4th series, vol. XII, 1880, pp. 28–32; A. Tindley, '"The Iron Duke": land reclamation and public relations in Sutherland, 1868–95', *Historical Research*, May 2009, vol. 82, no. 216, pp. 303–19.
10. McDonald (1880), op. cit. (note 9), pp. 32–44 (quote from p. 34).
11. Ibid., pp. 37, 42–48; Lane (1980), op. cit. (note 3), pp. 93–96.
12. *Engineering*, 10 December 1875, p. 453.
13. Tindley (2009), op. cit. (note 9), pp. 308, 311–13.
14. McDonald (1880), op. cit. (note 9), pp. 36–37.
15. *The Engineer*, 24 July 1874, p. 82; McDonald (1880), op. cit. (note 9), p. 42.
16. *Engineering*, 10 December 1875, p. 453.
17. A. Fenton, *Scottish country life* (1999), pp. 86–92.
18. G. E. Fussell, *The farmer's tools* (1981), pp. 165–73.
19. Highland and Agricultural Society of Scotland, op. cit. (note 2), p. 153; Fenton (1999), op. cit. (note 17), p. 92.
20. W. S. Hamilton, 'The most economical method of threshing grain combined with efficiency', *Transactions of the Highland and Agricultural Society of Scotland* (1882), 4th series, vol. xiv, pp. 133–36 (quote from p. 136).
21. Fussell (1982), (note 18), p. 176.
22. Hamilton (1882), op. cit. (note 20), pp. 137–38.
23. Marshall, Sons & Company Limited, *1907 Catalogue of portable engines, traction engines, thrashing machines, straw elevators, straw trussers, etc.*, publication no. 393 (1907), p. 34.
24. St J. V. Day, J. Mayer, J. Paton and J. Ferguson, *Notices of some of the principal manufactures of the west of Scotland* (1876), pp. 134–36 (quote from p. 134).
25. T. McTaggart, *Pioneers of heavy haulage* (1985), pp. 11–13.
26. Carter (1979), op. cit. (note 3), p. 82.
27. McTaggart (1985), op. cit. (note 25), pp. 13–65.

McTaggart's book is distinguished by a large number of photographs illustrating Road Engines and Kerr's road locomotives tackling an impressive range of heavy haulage tasks.

28. G. F. A. Gilbert, *Burrell style 1900–1932* (1994), ch. 13, 'Abstract of the specifications'.

29. D. Tew, *Traction engines and the law* (Birmingham, 2nd edition 1988), p. 10.

30. *The Motor World*, 15 July 1905, pp. 619–20, 623. At this time the term 'steam motor' was often used as an abbreviation for 'steam motor tractor'.

31. Aveling & Porter Limited, *Steam road rolling* (1907; facsimile edition, 1981), p. 50.

32. A. R. Thomas and J. L. Thomas, *An album of 'Sentinel' works photographs, No. 1 Standards and Supers* (1992), appendix, 'List of numbers and owners', pp. 105–106.

33. Aveling & Porter Limited (1907; 1981), op. cit. (note 31), pp. 58–65.

34. *The Berwickshire Advertiser*, 14 April 1908, p. 8.

35. H. Davies, *From tracks to motorways* (2006), pp. 85–92 provides a comprehensive survey of the development of road surfaces during the period of growth in mechanised transport.

36. *The Motor World*, 16 January 1913, p. 76.

37. Brown (2008), op. cit. (note 8), pp. 140 and 152.

38. J. Pease, *The history of J & H McLaren of Leeds* (2003), pp. 33–36. A copy of the letter to J. & H. McLaren, dated 12 August 1889, concerning the purchase of the Fowler ploughing engines and other equipment is held in the Scottish Life Archive [NMS W.MS.1996.19.25]. The information about the other engines bought by Turnbull is contained in the Alan Duke engine lists for Berwickshire, held by the Road Locomotive Society.

39. Invoice dated 27 August 1896 [NMS W.MS. 1996.19.3]; Memorandum (undated) [NMS W.MS.1996.19.1]; ledger 1907–1914, p. 61 (entries for threshing for Fairbairn at Walterstead, 9 and 25 October 1909) [NMS W.MS. 1996.19.2]; Shirlaw Allan & Company, 'Roup roll of sale of superior steam haulage & threshing plant … per instructions from the representatives of the late John Turnbull', 9 September 1919, [NMS W.MS. 1996.19.24].

40. *The Scotsman*, 16 August 1919, p. 11.

41. Anon., 'Raines of Stirling', *Scottish Traction Engine Society Newsletter*, January 1987, pp. 3–5; Alan Duke engine lists for Stirlingshire, held by the Road Locomotive Society; Stirling motor vehicle registration records via Jane Petrie, Stirling Archives (letter to the author 21 February 2008); Raines' history from Elma Lindsay, Stirling Local History Officer and Elspeth King, Stirling Smith Art Gallery and Museum (emails to the author, 20 and 28 March 2008).

42. Cecil Mowbray quoted in G. Reid, 'The man who flattened the Devil's Elbow', in *The Scots magazine*, September 1991, vol. 135, no. 6, pp. 599–601 (© The Scots Magazine, DC Thomson and Co. Ltd. www.scotsmagazine.com).

43. *The Engineer*, 5 January 1872, p. 18.

44. *Engineering*, 2 November 1894, p. 594.

45. *The Berwick Journal*, 23 April 1908, p. 7.

46. Brown (2008), op. cit. (note 8), p. 154; *The Implement and Machinery Review*, 1 August 1907, p. 471; The National Traction Engine Owners and Users Association, 'Report of a general meeting', 19 May 1920.

47. See, for example, D. K. Cameron, *The ballad and the plough: a portrait of the life of the old Scottish farmtouns* (1978), pp 194–96.

48. R. McEwen, *The life and rhymes of Robert McEwen: a self portrait* (2007), p. 8 (© Robert McEwan 2007).

49. J. S. Reid, *Mechanical Aberdeen* (1990), pp. 74–75.

50. Shetland Museum and Archives, photograph number G00037. The ploughing engine appears at the bottom right of the image, heavily cropped and showing only the top half of the boiler, engine and flywheel. It is nonetheless identifiable as a Fowler product of *c.*1870.

51. Cecil Mowbray quoted in G. Reid (in the *Scots Magazine*, September 1991, op. cit. (note 42), p. 602.

Chapter 4

KEEPING STEAM

Chapter 4

KEEPING STEAM

Preserving Scottish Traction Engines

As the working days of traction engines came to an end a small number of dedicated enthusiasts sought to preserve examples. An influential character was Ian Fraser, an engineer from Arbroath. In 1948 he acquired and then restored a Marshall steam tractor, made in 1915 and used first for haulage in Glasgow and then threshing in Angus until 1937. Fraser displayed his sense of humour by naming the engine 'Jingling Geordie', and for his own enjoyment he would steam the tractor around the town. Whilst building a new family house he prepared plans for an attractive engine-shed adjacent to it, suitable for the Marshall and a small steam locomotive from Dundee gasworks which he had also preserved. His neighbours objected to the local authority, but in a landmark legal case in 1959 Fraser won approval from the Secretary of State for Scotland to house and maintain these machines on his domestic property as part of his engineering hobby.[1] Encouraged by this success other private individuals were emboldened to make provision for keeping preserved traction engines at their homes.

Ian Fraser's saga prompted wide public interest including coverage in the national press. The Scottish Traction Engine Society was founded soon afterwards, and at its first Annual General Meeting in September 1961 he was elected President and Chairman. Other early traction engine preservationists included Freddy Forrest at Bonnybridge, Sir James Morrison-Low BT. and the Hon. Vere Cochrane, Jim Wood and Trevor Rees, and the Barrack brothers who were contractors based at Bridge of Don, Aberdeen. George Walker's farm at Townfoot, Uddingston, became a hub for Society activity from the mid-1960s until 1974. Some members' engines were housed there, and informal events were held with these in steam.[2] Another key individual was Jimmy Houston, who provided practical knowledge to new engine owners, and later designed and built his own small traction engine 'Tigger'.

In 1963 the Society presented eleven traction engines at the Royal Highland Show in Edinburgh, and over the following four decades a series of public rallies were held

Above:

MARSHALL STEAM ROLLER

Marshall 10-ton single cylinder steam roller, no. 83452 of 1928, owned by Jim Wood and Trevor Rees. The photograph was taken c.1967 and shows the roller on its first outing in their ownership, a test run between Easter Moffat (near Airdrie) to Lochhill farm and back. Jimmy Houston is driving and Trevor Rees is steering.

(John R. Hume Collection)

Right:

FOWLER PLOUGHING ENGINE, 'SAM HIRD'

Fowler 1925 ploughing engine number 15405 with preservationists Vere Cochrane, Ian Fraser and Sir James Morrison-Low BT. standing beside it in 1962 after it had been rescued from the scrapyard. This had been one of the last ploughing engines to be used commercially in Scotland. In preservation it was named 'Sam Hird' in recognition of its owner who operated it in Fife in the late 1930s.

(© Sir James Morrison-Low BT.)

at Hamilton, New Lanark and Summerlee.[3] Since 2004 the Society's main event has been held at Balado Park, Kinross, with around two dozen traction engines appearing in steam there each May. Similar rallies have been held in the north-east since 1967 and two organisations are active there currently: the Deeside Steam and Vintage Club, and the Bon Accord Steam Engine Club formed in 1975. The Deeside club holds a rally and road run in August whilst Bon Accord presents a Steam and Vintage Fair at Castle Fraser near Inverurie in June. Over forty traction engines appeared there in 2010.[4] At all these shows, club members' engines can be seen in steam, sometimes giving rides to the public, or demonstrating wood-sawing or threshing. Such events, and shows held around the country by other agricultural and vintage vehicle clubs and museums, collectively present working traction engines to tens of thousands of people in Scotland every year.

Over the same period public museums in Scotland, whose guiding principle is the preservation of permanent collections which reflect the nation's heritage, have also acquired traction engines. As described previously National Museums Scotland has a small portable engine by Tuxford of Lincoln from 1886, and a 1907 Marshall traction engine (which is examined in detail in the next chapter). Glasgow Museums have three machines: a 1920 traction engine 'Pride of Endrick' by Ruston & Hornsby of Lincoln, a 1931 Aveling & Porter steam roller 'Dragon' which worked in Fife, and a 1916 Sentinel steam wagon made in Shrewsbury and used at a steel works in Sheffield. Glasgow also holds the partial chassis and

HAMILTON LOW PARKS RALLY

An impressive line up of traction engines at the Hamilton Low Parks Rally in 1972.

(John R. Hume Collection)

Left:

STEAM AT SUMMERLEE

1928 Fowler steam roller no. 17251, registration DS7206, and, behind it, Foster portable steam engine no. 14657 at a Summerlee Steam Day in 1991.

(John R. Hume Collection)

Below:

STEAM THRESHING DEMONSTRATION, KELSO, 2009

Spectators gather to watch the commencement of a steam-threshing demonstration at the Border Vintage Agricultural Association rally, Kelso, May 2009. A McLaren compound traction engine of 1918 is powering a 54-inch Garvie threshing mill made in 1952.

(© Rosy Hayward)

two-cylinder engine of one of Goldsworthy Gurney's 1830 steam drags mentioned in chapter 1. The National Museum's Marshall and Glasgow's Ruston are both notable for having worked at some time with Raines of Stirling. Summerlee Museum of Scottish Industrial Life has a 1928 Fowler steam roller from Peebles, Jimmy Houston's 'Tigger', and a large portable steam engine made by Foster of Lincoln in 1941 which was used in a sawmill near Gifford, East Lothian. Three further saw-mill engines are preserved: a 1942 Marshall portable engine at Grampian Transport Museum and two similar engines at Landmark Forest Adventure Park near Avie-more. The former Edinburgh City Council Marshall steam roller of 1930 is preserved in the Scottish Bus Museum at Lathalmond, and in a creative arrangement Angus Council have kept ownership of one of their Fowler steam rollers of 1930, 'King o' the road', whilst entrusting its care and maintenance to a local enthusiast

in return for the roller being available to appear at council events.[5] The only Scottish-made machine in a public collection in this country is the Glasgow-built Sentinel steam wagon of 1914 owned by Grampian Transport Museum at Alford. Andrew Lawson's steam tricycle noted in chapter 1 is also held by this museum. Extending this survey to English museums, two engines with Scottish histories are preserved there. The Science Museum owns the 1906 Foden traction engine 'Pride of Leven' which was used for contract threshing in Dunbartonshire and is currently stored near Swindon, and Ian Fraser's Marshall steam tractor 'Jingling Geordie' is now kept by Leicestershire Museums.

Allowing for their small number, these exhibits are fairly representative of the types and makes of portable engine, general purpose agricultural engine, steam roller and wagon used in Scotland. There remain, nonetheless, a number of gaps in the Scottish public collections, notably ploughing engines, road locomotives and showman's road locomotives. At a time when purchase funds for museum collections are scarce, it is difficult for them to acquire such machinery, but fortunately private enthusiasts have preserved examples of all these types in Scotland. Noteworthy examples include the 1925 Fowler ploughing engine 'Sam Hird' which was one of the last working ploughing engines in Scotland, the Fowler road locomotive 'Finella' of 1914 which has a long Aberdeenshire history, and Burrell showman's road locomotive 'Dolphin' of 1925. There are many good examples too of traction engines, road rollers and steam wagons with Scottish working histories which are

privately preserved here. There is of course the possibility that such engines can at any time be sold to collectors outside Scotland, and like much movable heritage the nation's traction engine heritage is thus always at risk to some extent.[6] Recently, however, Scottish enthusiasts have instead added to that stock, returning engines with previous Scottish working histories (such as the 1925 Aveling & Porter traction engine 'Wizard' which worked for Moray County Highways),[7] or acquiring engines new to Scotland which are similar to machines once used here. Both are to be welcomed, especially when they are presented subsequently for public enjoyment at shows and rallies.

The most significant lack in both public and private collections in Britain is Scottish-built engines, with the exception of Grampian Transport Museum's Sentinel steam wagon noted previously, and a portable engine by A. & W. Smith & Company of Glasgow which worked in Latvia and is now preserved privately in England.[8] It is good to be able to note however that some more Scottish machines have been located overseas. As we saw earlier comparatively few were made and so it is not surprising that only a few survive. Those that do have considerable intrinsic value as rare evidence of this specialised sector of Scottish engineering practice, and as a physical reminder of the extent of Scotland's engineering exports and interests in the nineteenth and early twentieth centuries. All these artefacts, and the themes they embody, merit further research. Examples include part of the frame and the engine of a Thomson road steamer in Australia[9] where there are also two

portable engines made by T. M. Tennant & Company.[10] In Africa there is a Bow McLachlan traction engine, and in New Zealand the remains of a ploughing engine by Aveling and John Gray of Uddingston,[11] both of which have already been noted in chapter 1. It is exciting to consider that other examples of Scottish-built engines – a complete road steamer perhaps, or one of Alexander Chaplin's early traction engines, or another Polmadie Sentinel – may yet remain to be discovered elsewhere around the globe.

Left:

ROAD ROLLING IN 1961

Preservationists enjoyed finding and recording engines still at work. Here one of Perthshire County Council's Fowler compound steam rollers has been photographed near Kirkmichael in summer sunshine in July 1961.

(© Sir James Morrison-Low Bᴛ.)

Next page:

GRAMPIAN TRANSPORT MUSEUM'S 1914 SENTINEL STEAM WAGON

Grampian Transport Museum's 1914 Sentinel steam wagon, no. 753, registration V3057, on the road near Alford.

(© Grampian Transport Museum, Aberdeen)

References

1. I. N. Fraser, *The Arbroath affair* (1961), pp. 9–29.
2. Anon., 'Some thoughts on the President', *Scottish Traction Engine Society Newsletter*, vol. 3, no. 1, March 2010.
3. Ibid.
4. www.bonaccordsteamclub.co.uk [accessed March 2011]
5. R. Weir, 'King o' the road', *Vintage Spirit*, no. 102, January 2011, pp 36–39.
6. J. R. Hume, 'Transport and museums', in K. Veitch (ed.) *Scottish life and society: a compendium of Scottish ethnology, vol. 8, Transport and communications* (2009), pp. 891, 894.
7. *Old Glory*, November 2009, pp. 24–25.
8. Anon., 'A Glasgow portable?', *Steaming*, vol. 43, no. 1, 1999, p. 32; J. B. True and B. Johnson, *The traction engine register* (2008), p. 76.
9. This road steamer was probably made by Tennant: Tony Brown, road locomotive historian, personal communication 4 March 2010.
10. *Old Glory*, May 2005, p 27; July 2005, p. 28.
11. *Old Glory*, March 2010, p. 26.

Chapter 5

MUSEUM STEAM

Chapter 5

MUSEUM STEAM

The Marshall Traction Engine in National Museums Scotland

THE Royal Scottish Museum – predecessor of the National Museums Scotland – had long recognised the place of the traction engine in the history of engineering, and the need to represent this in its collections. Space constraints in the Victorian museum building in Chambers Street in Edinburgh precluded the museum from obtaining much full-size machinery and so, like many other museums at the time, drawings, photographs, components or models were collected instead. Among these the following items stand out. The earliest era of steam-powered road transport was represented by a fine model purchased in 1905 of Nicolas-Joseph Cugnot's steam vehicle intended for the haulage of artillery, first paraded in Paris in 1771.[1] In 1926 the museum commissioned a replica of the working concept model of the steam vehicle which William Murdoch built between 1784 and 1786.[2] Three years later the museum acquired two photographs dated December 1863 showing a 15-horsepower traction engine made by Alexander Chaplin & Company in Glasgow.[3] These photographs and the Murdoch model are illustrated in chapter 1. In 1950 a one-eighth scale working model traction engine of *circa* 1910 was acquired, complete with a set of tools and lamps.[4] The following year the first full-size item was collected. This was the little 1886 Tuxford portable engine[5] illustrated in chapter 3, and its diminutive size allowed it to be displayed in the Victorian Engineering gallery.

During the late 1980s a new store for the museum was established in Granton, on the northern side of Edinburgh, making possible the acquisition of a range of larger engines and machines. In 1987 the museum's Department of Science, Technology and Working Life acquired a full-size Marshall traction engine[6] from a private collector near Stirling. The engine then entered into a new phase of its life as a museum exhibit representing the simple, heavy steam engines used in road haulage and agriculture in Scotland in the decades around 1900. Research carried out more recently on the museum's engine in connection with the completion of restoration for its centenary in 2007 has made it possible to piece together a fascinating early history. These findings are set out in this chapter, which takes the form of a biography of the Marshall, exploring its design origins, manufacture, working life, and restoration twice over.

Marshall of Gainsborough: makers of the museum's traction engine

The museum's traction engine was made in 1907 by Marshall, Sons & Company Limited at their Britannia Ironworks in Gainsborough, England. In the early twentieth century Marshall was amongst the largest agricultural engineering manufacturers in Britain, and one of a number of such firms concentrated in the grain-producing regions of Lincolnshire and East Anglia. Originally established in 1848 as general millwrights, the company went on to develop a significant trade in threshing machines and steam engines to power them, both throughout Britain and around the world. These were however only a part of Marshall's production, which extended to industrial products like stationary boilers and large steam engines for powering factories and mills, and even plant for gold-dredging and tea-processing.[7] Thus could the firm claim in a catalogue of 1907 that their total output was 'over 120,000 Engines, Boilers, Thrashing [sic] Machines, &c., made and supplied'. At this time the Britannia Ironworks covered 30 acres and employed 4000 men.[8]

The first Marshall traction engine was made in 1876 and had a horizontal single-cylinder engine mounted on a frame under a locomotive-type boiler. By the following year, the more common layout had been adopted by Marshall, with the engine mounted on top of the boiler and driving through a gear train to the rear wheels.[9] Marshall's general purpose traction engines were made in four sizes: 5-, 6-, 7- and 8-nominal horsepower with either single or twin compound cylinders. The former were far more well-liked by buyers. In the quarter century between 1888 and 1913, effectively the hey-day of traction engine production, five hundred 6-horsepower single-cylinder traction engines (the same size and basic design as the museum's engine) were made by the company, compared with only seventy-four 6-horsepower compound engines. Combined production of 7- and 8-horsepower engines was about the same as the total for the 6-horsepower size over the same period, with a much smaller number of 5-horsepower engines also produced.[10] The 6-horsepower size was clearly the most popular, sufficiently powerful to haul most loads and drive most threshing mills, and, for the British market, small enough to be reasonably manoeuvrable in country lanes and farmyards from Cornwall to Scotland.

'Of high-class construction throughout …': making the Marshall traction engine

Describing their general purpose traction engines, suitable for road haulage and powering machinery, Marshall wrote in its 1907 catalogue that

... they are of high-class construction throughout and embody in their manufacture the most modern improvements, combined with strength, durability, economy and handiness of working. The materials are the very best for their various purposes, and the workmanship throughout of the highest order.[11]

By this time, traction engines were quite elegant in outline too, in contrast with earlier machines which often looked ungainly. This was largely as a result of the efforts of the traction engine designer William Fletcher who had worked for a number of the leading English firms including Marshall. He wrote:

Beauty of design is more easily appreciated than described. It consists of no alteration in the principle, neither does it affect the internal details of the engine, but it is brought about by an expenditure of drawing-office care in the arrangement of the parts, which gives to the whole a symmetrical and <u>simple appearance</u> [Fletcher's emphasis].

Every detail is made to possess perfect and graceful proportions and a pleasing outline, and the shape of one part is not allowed to be out of accord with any other part, and in no case is <u>real efficiency</u> [ditto] *sacrificed thereby.*[12]

MARSHALL CATALOGUE

Description of general purpose traction engine from 1907 catalogue.

(© Museum of English Rural Life, University of Reading)

GENERAL PURPOSE TRACTION ENGINE

Our latest Traction Engines are now fitted with the following **important improvements :—**

The First Motion Gearing is arranged inside the Bearings.
One Clutch and Lever changes both speeds alternately.
Compensating Gear fitted with 4 Pinions.
The Countershaft is square, dispensing with keys or feathers.
The Speeds have been increased to 2 and 4 miles per hour respectively.
Pump inside the Tender—ease of access by the Driver.
Special strong Tank to take haulage strain.
Extra large Travelling Wheels, with Special Section heavy steel Tee Rings.

 Over **120,000** Engines, Boilers, Thrashing Machines, &c., made and supplied

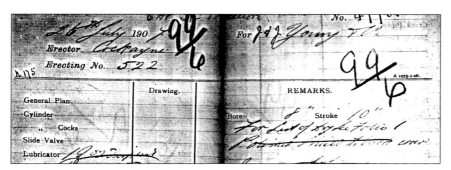

MARSHALL SPECIFICATION

Header from Marshall 47731 specification.

(© National Museums Scotland)

Within the home market, traction engines were most often ordered singly, as few British contractors, farmers or local authorities operated on such a large scale or had access to finance to allow the purchase of more than one engine, or set of ploughing or threshing tackle, at a time. Hence engines tended to be made in response to a specific order from a customer (or sometimes a selling agent), allowing their individual requirements to be met. This custom-built approach meant that similar machines in Marshall's erecting workshop would often exhibit detail differences to a greater or lesser degree. Mass production techniques were therefore rarely seen in British traction engine factories, although the larger firms like Marshall would manufacture components which could be standardised (such as wheels, cylinders, gears, boiler fittings and even whole boilers) in quantity to be held in stock. Export production could be another matter however; for example, the nearby firm Ruston Proctor of Lincoln produced 990 near-identical traction engines in batches for sale to the huge grain producing estates in Argentina between 1903 and 1913.[13]

Contemporary information and surviving documentation relating to the museum's traction engine allows us to sketch out the procedures and processes in the Marshall factory at this time. Each traction engine made by the firm had comprehensive details of its specification set out by a registrar in a bound ledger, but unfortunately the volume for the museum's engine is not available.[14] The various components of the engine – ranging from cylinder and boiler to small items like the lubricator and water gauge – were listed, and against each there was space for the identification numbers of the drawings used in their manufacture, with a further column giving leading dimensions, finishes, and other details. A copy survives of the pages from the note-book used by the registrar in compiling information to be included in the final specifications for the museum's traction engine, and is dated 26 July 1907.[15] The customer for whom the engine was to be made is identified as 'J. & J. Young & Co'. The erector's surname was Cockayne, and the erecting number was 522. The engine number is entered as 47731. The erector was in charge of

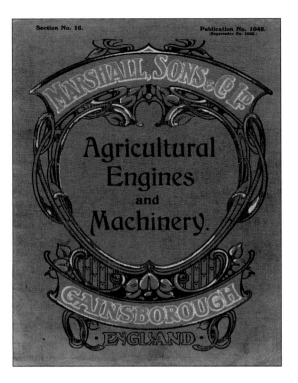

Section No. 16.   Publication No. 1048.
                                   (Supersedes No. 1005.)

MARSHALL, SONS & C?

Agricultural
Engines
and
Machinery.

GAINSBOROUGH

· ENGLAND ·

brought together and assembled in the engine erecting shop. In the Britannia Works all sorts of machines jostled together in the erecting shop; enormous stationary steam engines, smaller portable steam engines, together with traction engines and steam rollers. The erecting shop was a tall building with a travelling gantry crane running at high level along its length. This crane was used to bring the major components together at the assembly location where the erector and his gang worked. The components were lifted onto the growing engine (where necessary using hand cranes which ran at ground level along the sides of the workshop), being hand-fitted and adjusted as required by the erecting team as they were assembled together. When the engine was finished it went to the testing shed. Here it was put in steam, the power output measured, and everything checked to see that it operated correctly. This was followed by a road test, and if all was well, the engine went to the paint shop before final despatch.

Marshall traction engines made in the 1900s were usually painted maroon with bright red wheels.

Ornate narrow striping, or lining, was then applied by skilled craftsmen, in black, white, red or yellow to complement the body colour. Some of the lining on flat plate work and adjacent to the polished brass boiler bands was similar in style to that applied to railway locomotives. Other decoration, especially on the wheels and under gear, consisted of freehand patterns and curves which more closely resembled that traditionally applied to horse-drawn carts and wagons.

A distinguishing feature of Marshall traction engines

the small team (a couple of men and possibly an apprentice or boy to provide assistance) that assembled each engine. The erecting number was assigned when the instruction was given to start assembly, and remained the means of identifying the machine in the factory until it was complete when an engine number was allocated. The engine number was then engraved on a brass maker's plate fixed to the engine, and provided an essential reference for the subsequent supply of spare parts.

All the constituent parts, made in separate departments spread across the extensive factory site, were

MARSHALL, SONS & COMPANY LIMITED

ERECTING SHOP FROM MARSHALL 1907 CATALOGUE

Two views from Marshall's 1907 catalogue illustrating the engine erecting shop at the Britannia Ironworks, Gainsborough. The firm's large product range is evident, with stationary and portable steam engines greatly outnumbering traction engines. The boiler barrel, hornplates and tender for a part-assembled traction engine can be seen at the very front of the left-hand image, with the bolt holes for the cylinder base visible next to the large hole in the top of the smokebox for the chimney base. These photographs would have been taken on a Saturday afternoon or Sunday when no one was at work.

(© Museum of English Rural Life, University of Reading)

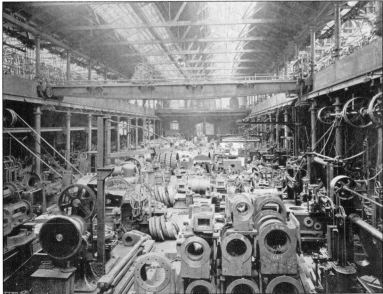

MARSHALL TRACTION ENGINE

Rear view illustrating the ornate 'Show' finish applied to 'Sir Hector'.

(© National Museums Scotland)

was the large transfer applied usually to the side of the boiler barrel. Here a figure of Britannia, Marshall's imperial trademark, stands symbolically on a large gear wheel, surrounded by reproductions of some of the hundreds of prize medals the firm had been awarded at agricultural and engineering shows around the globe.

With even the standard level of finish, Marshall engines were thus striking and colourful, but the quality of finish could be enhanced for engines that were destined for exhibition at trade shows and agricultural fairs, making them more attractive to potential customers. Some purchasers requested this at extra cost if they were especially proud of their engine. Then extra attention would be paid to getting an even more shiny finish on the paintwork, more ornate lining applied, and bare metal items like the valve gear, hubcaps and controls burnished to a shine. Such finish was described by Marshall as 'Show' or even 'Royal Show' depending on the amount of effort directed to it, and reflecting their perception of a hierarchy of occasions which justified such additional work.

The specification for the museum's engine includes details of a number of items addressing the customer's particular requirements. Marshall 47731 was to be fitted with a name-plate identifying the owner as J. & J. Young, Timber Merchants, Oakley. The engine itself was to be named 'Sir Hector', and this (presumably on a brass plate) was to be fixed to a wood block on the side of the boiler barrel. An injector was ordered for supplying the boiler with water, in addition to the crankshaft-driven pump supplied as standard. Rim brakes were to be fitted to the rear wheels. Marshall traction engines usually had only a simple band brake acting on a small diameter brake drum on one rear wheel; rim brakes comprised large wooden brake blocks which acted on a larger diameter on the inside rim of both rear wheels and hence were much more effective at braking or holding the engine. In addition the cylinder was to have a 'Polished Shield to back cover' and a semi circle brass name plate 'Marshall Sons & Co' mounted on the smokebox door. The 'Finish' is noted as 'Maroon & Lined Show'.

These last three points suggest that Marshall 47731 was destined for exhibition, particularly the application of 'Show' finish and the brass plate with maker's name on the smokebox door. Marshall traction engines usually had an unadorned smokebox door, so this addition was an effective way of emphasising their identity to show visitors and prospective purchasers. As we saw in chapter 2, Marshall was among the exhibitors at the Highland and Agricultural Society's show held in Edinburgh in 1907, showing a 6-horsepower single-cylinder traction engine together with four threshing mills. Although this is the same size as the museum's engine, it is not clear how it could be the same one, as the Edinburgh show was two and a half weeks earlier than the 26 July date given for 47731 in Marshall's registrar's notebook. Nor does Marshall's catalogue entry for the Highland Show mention non-standard rim brakes or additional injector in the specification for the engine on show: *'Traction Engine, single cylinder, 6 nominal HP, with water-lifter and winding-drum, fitted with steel gearing for two travelling speeds – Price £460; extras as per Catalogue.'*[16]

MARSHALL TRACTION ENGINE

Above: Brass maker's nameplate on the smokebox door.

Below: Britannia transfer with show medals.
(© National Museums Scotland)

In the absence of clear evidence demonstrating how Marshall 47731 might in fact have been exhibited in Edinburgh, there are three other possible explanations for its 'Show' appearance. Perhaps J. & J. Young simply wanted a highly finished engine, maybe as an advertisement for their business, and had been prepared to order this specially. Maybe they visited the Edinburgh show, were impressed by Marshall's stand and 6-horsepower traction engine there, and decided to order a similar engine for themselves. Marshall must have put on a good display, as the show report in the *North British Agriculturist* described their stand as 'a very high-class exhibit'.[17] Or perhaps 47731 was exhibited at another show elsewhere that summer and then delivered to J. & J. Young.

'Sir Hector' at work

Oakley, where Marshall 47731 first worked, is in the south-west corner of Fife. In 1907 the gently rolling countryside surrounding the village was interspersed with coal mines. As timber merchants, J. & J. Young may have been involved in the supply of pit props for the collieries, or hauling logs from forest to sawmill for processing and then delivering cut timber for building and manufacture. It must have been quite a prosperous business, as Young's owned two other traction engines at this time. Both had been purchased new, the first in 1883 and the second, named 'The Rover', in 1906. Another new engine, a steam tractor, followed in 1912.[18] All these were made by John Fowler & Company of Leeds, so 'Sir

Hector', as a Marshall product, must have stood out. The rear wheel-rim brakes fitted to 'Sir Hector' suggest it was intended to be used for haulage (rather than for driving stationary machinery), as these were an important fitting for a traction engine expected to move heavy loads in undulating country.

By early 1921 'Sir Hector' had been sold to Raines & Company Limited, the large-scale threshing contractors operating out of Bridgehaugh, Stirling. We know this because it was registered by Raines with the local authority on 1 February that year, receiving the registration mark MS3081.[19] How long the engine had been with Raines, or whether there was another owner between Young and Raines, is not known. 'Sir Hector' also carries a cast brass plate on its tender side proclaiming membership of the Scottish Traction Engine Owners and Users Association. Although we cannot be certain when this plate was fixed to the engine, it is certain that Raines (and likely Young) would have been members. As we have seen already Richard Raines was at one time Chairman of the Association and would no doubt have wished his company's engines to wear the brass membership plate with pride. Unfortunately, no photographs have yet been found illustrating 'Sir Hector' in either firm's ownership.

When Raines gave up contract threshing and then auctioned its engines in August 1945, Marshall 47731 was bought by James Kenny of Stirling; by now the engine was without its nameplate. In 1948 the engine was sold to Jock Mackay at Whins of Milton, near Stirling.[20] Jock was an engineer and steam enthusiast, and Mar-

shall 47731 thus became one of the first traction engines to be preserved in Scotland (concurrent with Ian Fraser's Marshall 'Jingling Geordie'). Jock and his wife Peggy then restored the engine, repainting it green with yellow wheels. In the course of restoring Marshall 47731 they met up with Wattie Tough who had driven it for 11 years whilst working for Raines. Wattie presented them with the nameplate for 'Sir Hector' which he had kept as a souvenir of his time with the engine.[21] Jock sold Marshall 47731 to the Royal Museum of Scotland in September 1987.

'Sir Hector' comes to the museum

The museum's intention had always been to demonstrate its traction engine in steam, and so an early concern was the fitness of the engine for this. When the museum acquired the engine, it had not been steamed for some time, and so the boiler inspector required the boiler barrel to be stripped of its thin sheet metal covering thus allowing its condition to be thoroughly assessed.

'Sir Hector' was now eighty years old and not surprisingly the boiler was found to be nearing the end of its

Below:

MARSHALL THRESHING AT DUNBLANE SHOW

The engine as owned by Jock Mackay.

(© National Museums Scotland)

Below:

MEMBERSHIP PLATE FOR THE SCOTTISH TRACTION ENGINE OWNERS & USERS ASSOCIATION.

This was fixed to the side of the coal bunker on 'Sir Hector'.

(© National Museums Scotland)

serviceable life; its working pressure had been lowered from the original figure of 140 pounds per square inch (psi) to 100 psi in the mid-1970s. Initially it had been hoped to put the engine into working order by the summer of 1989, but as investigations proceeded the museum decided the correct approach would be to undertake a thorough overhaul. Ultimately a decision was made to renew the corroded inner firebox; removing the original one meant that the whole interior of the boiler was able to be seen and corroded areas identified for repair. A specialist boiler repairer in West Yorkshire tackled this job, of which making and fitting the new firebox was the most complicated part. Other plate work and boiler fittings were repaired or refurbished, and new fire tubes were fitted. At the end of this work the boiler could again be steamed safely at its original working pressure.

Attention had also to be given to the mechanical components. The engine had evidently been worked hard during its commercial life, with very worn drive gears in particular testifying to many miles travelled on the road. There is evidence of the rivets fastening the spectacle plate near the main bearings having been hammered up tight as a running repair; their coming loose was a likely result of the strains and vibration caused by sustained and arduous operation. A piece had also broken out of the end of the engine's cast-iron trunk guide at some time, although the cause of this is not known.

The largest of the many engineering tasks undertaken was the cutting of new gears by a firm in Ayrshire. Bearings were replaced and worn components built up with new metal. Respect for the original design was a key precept for all this work, but in two areas there were important practical deviations from Marshall's 1907 specification. Rubber strakes (the narrow plates angled across the surface of the driving wheels to give grip) were fitted to soften the ride on hard roads, in place of the thin iron strakes fitted when the engine was new. A more sensitive regulator valve was fitted to the engine to allow finer throttle control. This was designed and made by Hamish Orr-Ewing, who was the owner of another restored Marshall traction engine, and helps tame the characteristic habit of Marshall engines rearing up on their hind wheels when starting and then falling hard back down on their front wheels.

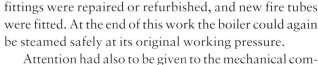

MARSHALL STEAM TRACTION ENGINE

The damaged trunk guide and, left, re-worked rivets testifying to a hard working life.

(© National Museums Scotland)

BEFORE AND AFTER

Photographs show the engine stripped, with conservator Chris Cockburn, and the Boiler Inspector in 1988, and with Chris polishing the engine in 2007.

(© National Museums Scotland)

Early in the restoration the museum thought the engine was painted dark blue, having found traces of this colour on metal-work as the engine was dismantled. This blue effect may well have been the mill scale on platework underneath the original paint, as Marshall's registrar's notes for the engine clearly indicate it was to be painted maroon. Expert advice was sought from the Road Locomotive Society – a long-established educational charity dedicated to researching traction engine history – as to the correct colours and lining details for 'Show' finish in 1907. In response, pages of notes and detailed sketches were supplied by Richard Willcox, the Society's Liveries Officer.

With changing museum priorities over the years, and the consequent ebb and flow of budgets, the restoration took twenty years to complete. It proved to be one of the most complex engineering restoration projects ever undertaken by National Museums Scotland and it was achieved through teamwork between curators and conservation staff. The impetus for final completion of the project was the engine's impending centenary in 2007, linked to research in the museum revealing in late 2005 that a very similar engine, if not 'Sir Hector', had been displayed at the Highland Show in 1907. The possibility of attendance at the Highland Show in 2007 provided the team with a deadline to aim for, and so the museum's engineering conservator set to work, reassembling, testing and painting 'Sir Hector' before its elaborate 'Show' lining and Marshall Britannia transfer was applied by a local signwriter. Last of all, the engine was varnished, with this and the painting being carried out authentically by hand-brushing rather than using modern spray-painting equipment.

'Sir Hector' was then ready for its debut on 21 June 2007 at the Royal Highland Showground at Ingliston, near Edinburgh. With this in mind the National Museum of Rural Life (one of the family of museums that makes up National Museums Scotland) decided that its stand at the Show would take threshing as its theme and present the newly-restored engine driving a small threshing mill made by R. Scott of Strichen. The engine and the mill attracted huge interest from visitors, especially children, and those old enough to remember such scenes from their younger days. Many anecdotes were shared with museum staff concerning steam threshing from Ayrshire to the Black Isle, reflecting its impact on peoples' memories, and even the affection with which such machines are still remembered.

'Sir Hector' has since attended a number of rallies and shows, including the Scottish Traction Engine Society's event at Balado in Kinross-shire, Selkirk Vintage Rally, 'Harvest Home' at the National Museum of Rural Life in Lanarkshire, and 'Magnificent Machines' at the National Museum of Flight in East Lothian.

The engine continues to offer exciting possibilities of acting as a travelling ambassador for National Museums Scotland, bringing a key item from its collections to communities across the nation.

References

1. National Museums Scotland [NMS] T.1905.40. Cugnot's original vehicle is preserved in the Conservatoire National des Arts et Métiers, Paris.
2. [NMS T.1926.12]. Murdoch's original model is preserved in the collections of Birmingham Museums & Art Gallery.
3. [NMS T.1929.401.1 and 2].
4. [NMS T.1950.6]. The model is notable for having been made by a former employee of one of the leading English traction engine makers, Robey and Company of Lincoln. It appears not to represent any particular proto-type, but looks more like a Burrell traction engine than a Robey.
5. [NMS T.1951.13].
6. [NMS T.1988.17].
7. M. R. Lane, *The story of the Britannia Ironworks: William Marshall and Sons, Gainsborough* (1993)
8. Marshall, Sons & Company Limited, *1907 Catalogue of portable engines, traction engines, thrashing machines, straw elevators, straw trussers, etc.*, publication no. 393 (1907), rear cover.
9. M. R. Lane, op. cit. (note 7), pp. 20–22.
10. Ibid., pp. 55–57.
11. Marshall, Sons & Company Limited, op. cit. (note 8), p. 17.
12. W. Fletcher, *The history and development of steam locomotion on common roads* (1891), pp. 277–278.
13. R. Brooks, *Lincolnshire engines worldwide* (n.d.), pp. 1, 24.
14. These bound specifications are described as 'building books' in the catalogues of the Museum of English Rural Life, University of Reading, where a number of surviving Marshall records are housed [reference TR MAR MP1]. The building book covering the period during which the museum's traction engine was made is missing; the other building books are split between the Museum of English Rural Life and R. H. Crawford, Boston. The Museum of English Rural Life also holds some of Marshall's prod-uction registers, although the register covering the period during which the museum's traction engine was made is missing too.
15. Photocopy in NMS Object File [T.1988.17]. This was supplied to the museum on 1 February 1988 by Major H. D. Marshall of Track Marshall, Gainsborough, who then had custody of Mar-shall's traction engine records. Major Marshall's letter accompanying the photocopy explains that each entry in the note book (which has the same format as the building book) was crossed off by the registrar as he entered the information into the 'register' – the term Major Marshall used to describe the building books.
16. Highland and Agricultural Society of Scotland, *Implement catalogue, Edinburgh Show*, 1907, p. 103.
17. *The North British Agriculturist*, 11 July 1907, p. 443.
18. Alan Duke engine lists for Fife, held by the Road Locomotive Society.
19. Stirling motor vehicle registration records via Jane Petrie, Stirling Archives (letter to the author 21 February 2008).
20. Alan Duke engine lists for Stirlingshire, held by the Road Locomotive Society.
21. Anon., 'Jock Mackay', *Scottish Traction Engine Society Newsletter*, November 1983, p. 6.

Bibliography and References

ARCHIVES AND COLLECTIONS

Caithness Horizons, Thurso: photographic collections.

Department of Science and Technology, National Museums Scotland: A–Z of Scottish engineering firms, technical object files and accession registers.

Grampian Transport Museum, Alford: photographic collections.

Museum of English Rural Life, University of Reading: Marshall, Sons & Company Limited and J. & H. McLaren trade literature.

Record Office for Leicestershire, Leicester and Rutland: Alexander Chaplin & Company business archive.

Road Locomotive Society: Alan Duke county lists of traction engines.

Scottish Life Archive, National Museums Scotland: photographic and manuscript collections.

Shetland Museum and Archives, Lerwick: photographic collections

Signal Tower Museum, Arbroath: Alexander Shanks & Company business archive and trade literature.

Stirling Archives: motor vehicle registration records.

NEWSPAPERS, PERIODICALS AND REFERENCE BOOKS

The Berwick Journal
The Berwickshire Advertiser
The British Farmer's Magazine
Chambers's Encyclopaedia
Civil Engineer and Architect's Journal
The Engineer
Engineering
Historical Research
The Implement and Machinery Review
Mechanics' Magazine
The Motor World
The North British Agriculturist
Old Glory
Patent specifications
Road Locomotive Society Journal
The Scotsman
Scottish Traction Engine Society Newsletter
Steaming: the magazine of the National Traction Engine Trust
Transactions of the Highland and Agricultural Society of Scotland [THASS]
Vintage Spirit

BOOKS AND ARTICLES

ANON. (1864), *Lord Kinnaird's model farm: a visit to Millhill* [and] *The steam plough in the Carse of Gowrie* (Dundee: Dundee Advertiser).

ANON. (1877), 'On implements selected for trial: Part 1 Fisken steam cultivating machinery', *THASS*, 4th series, vol. IX, 1877.

ANON. (1900), 'Trial of oil-engines', *THASS*, 5th series, vol. XII, 1900.

ANON. (1905a), 'Trials of agricultural motors and dung-distributors', *THASS*, 5th series, vol. XVII, 1905.

ANON. (1905b), 'The Thornycroft five-ton lorry', *The Motor World*, 4 November 1905.

ANON. (1906a), 'Trials of suction gas-producer plants', *THASS*, 5th series, vol. XVIII, 1906.

ANON. (1906b), 'The Glasgow show', *The Motor World*, 17 March 1906.

ANON. (1911), 'The late Mr Andrew Gilchrist, J.P., Carvenom', *Extract from East of Fife Record*, 24 August 1911 [NMS W.MS.1985.52.2].

ANON. (1983), 'Jock Mackay', *Scottish Traction Engine Society Newsletter*, November 1983.

ANON. (1987), 'Raines of Stirling', *Scottish Traction Engine Society Newsletter*, January 1987.

ANON. (1999), 'A Glasgow portable?', *Steaming*, vol. 43, no. 1, 1999.

ANON. (2010), 'Some thoughts on the President', *Scottish Traction Engine Society Newsletter*, vol. 3, no. 1, March 2010.

AVELING & PORTER LIMITED (1907), *Steam road rolling* (Rochester: Aveling & Porter Limited, 1907); facsimile published by the Road Locomotive Society, 1981).

BOURNE, J. (1856), *A catechism of the steam engine* (London: Longman, Brown, Green & Longmans, 4th edition 1856).

BROOKS, R. (n.d.), *Lincolnshire engines worldwide* (Lincoln: Lincolnshire County Council, n.d.).

BROWN, J. (2008), *Steam on the farm: a history of agricultural steam engines 1800 to 1950* (Marlborough: Crowood Press, 2008).

CAMERON, D. K. (1978), *The ballad and the plough: a portrait of the life of the old Scottish farmtouns* (London: Victor Gollancz, 1978).

CARTER, I. (1979), *Farm life in northeast Scotland* (Edinburgh: John Donald Publishers, 1979).

CLARK, D. K. (1864), *The exhibited machinery of 1862: a cyclopaedia of the machinery represented at the International Exhibition* (London: Day and Son, 1864).

CLARK, R. H. (1963), The development of the English steam wagon (Norwich: Goose & Son, 1963).

CLYDESDALE, J. (2004), *Perth's first motor vehicle* (Perth: John Clydesdale, 2004).

COLLINS, E. J. T. (1996), *Power availability and agricultural productivity in England and Wales*

1840–1939 (University of Reading: Rural History Centre, Discussion paper no. 1, 1996).

COMMISSIONERS OF THE INTERNATIONAL EXHIBITION OF 1862, *Illustrated catalogue of the industrial department*, British division, vol. 1 (London: 1862).

CRUICKSHANK, J. (1935), *Changes in the agricultural industry of Aberdeenshire in the last fifty years* (Aberdeen, 1935).

DAVIDSON, J. D. G. (ed.) (1984), *A short history: 1784–1984, Royal Highland and Agricultural Society of Scotland* (Edinburgh: Royal Highland and Agricultural Society of Scotland, 1984).

DAVIES, H. (2006), *From tracks to motorways* (Stroud: Tempus Publishing, 2006).

DAY, St J. V., MAYER, J., PATON, J., and FERGUSON, J. (1876), *Notices of some of the principal manufactures of the west of Scotland* (Glasgow, 1876).

DEWEY, P. (2008), *Iron harvests of the field: the making of farm machinery in Britain since 1800* (Lancaster: Carnegie Publishing, 2008).

DICKINSON, H. W. and JENKINS, R. (1927) *James Watt and the steam engine* (1927; facsimile edition London: Encore Editions, 1981).

DODDS, A. (1996), *Making cars* (Edinburgh: NMS Publishing Limited, 1996).

DUDGEON, J. S., LOGAN, A. S., MIDDLETON, J. and PATERSON, J. T. S. (1889), 'Report of the trials of steam engines at Glasgow 1888, by the judges', *THASS*, 5th series, vol. I, 1889.

EDGERTON, D. (2006), *The shock of the old* (London: Profile Books, 2006).

FENTON, A. (1999), *Scottish country life* (East Linton: Tuckwell Press, 1999).

FLETCHER, W. (1891), *The history and development of steam locomotion on common roads* (London: E. & F. N. Spon, 1891).

FLETCHER, W. (1904), *English and American steam carriages and traction engines* (1904; facsimile edition, Newton Abbot: David & Charles, 1973).

JOHN FOWLER & COMPANY (LEEDS) LIMITED (n.d.), *Road making machinery* (Leeds: John Fowler & Company [Leeds] Limited, n.d.), facsimile catalogue published by the Road Locomotive Society, n.d.).

FRASER, I. N. (1961), *The Arbroath affair* (Arbroath: T. Buncle & Company, 1961).

FUSSELL, G. E. (1981), *The farmer's tools* (London: Orbis Publishing, 1981)

GILBERT, G. F. A. (1994), *Burrell style 1900–1932* (Road Locomotive Society, 1994).

GILBERT, G. F. A. and OSBORNE, D. J. (n.d.), *Charles Burrell & Sons Ltd* (Thetford: Friends of the Charles Burrell Museum, n.d.).

GRAMPIAN TRANSPORT MUSEUM (1999), *The Craigievar Express* (Alford: Grampian Transport Museum, 3rd edition, 1999).

HAMILTON, W. S. (1882), 'The most economical method of threshing grain combined with efficiency', *THASS*, 1882, 4th series, vol. XIV.

HIGHLAND AND AGRICULTURAL SOCIETY OF SCOTLAND (1871), *THASS*, 4th series, vol. III, 1871, Appx A, 'Proceedings at General Meetings'.

– (1878), *Report on the present state of agriculture in Scotland* (Edinburgh: Highland and Agricultural Society of Scotland, 1878).

– (1907a), *Implement catalogue: Edinburgh Show, 1907*.

– (1907b), *THASS*, 5th series, vol. XIX, 1907, Appendix A, *Regulations for General Show at Edinburgh*.

– (1915), *Exhibition trial of motor tillage implements* (Edinburgh: Highland and Agricultural Society of Scotland, 1915).

HUGHES, W. J. (1972), *A century of traction engines* (London: Pan Books, 3rd edition 1972).

HUGHES, W. J. and THOMAS, J. L. (1973), 'The Sentinel': vol. 1 1875–1930 (Newton Abbot: David & Charles, 1973).

HUME, J. R. (2009), 'Transport and museums' in K. Veitch (ed.), *Scottish life and society: a compendium of Scottish ethnology, vol. 8, Transport and communications* (Edinburgh: John Donald, in association with The European Ethnological Research Centre, 2009).

HURST, K. A. (2004), *William Beardmore: 'Transport is the thing'* (Edinburgh: NMS Publishing Limited, 2004).

HUTCHINSON, S. (1863), *Fire and water versus corn and hay: an essay on the effects of steam cultivation* (London: Simpkin, 1863).

KENNEDY, B. (1990), *Demonstrations and trials of tractors 1904–1934* [Reprints from the trial reports in contemporary volumes of *Transactions of the Highland and Agricultural Society of Scotland*] (Banff: B. Kennedy, 1990).

LANE, M. R. (1976), *Pride of the road* (London: New English Library, 1976).

LANE, M. R. (1980), *The story of the Steam Plough Works: Fowlers of Leeds* (London: Northgate Publishing, 1980).

LANE, M. R. (1993), *The story of the Britannia Ironworks: William Marshall and Sons, Gainsborough* (London: Quiller Press, 1993).

LANE, M. R. (1999), *The story of the St Nicholas Works: a history of Charles Burrell and Sons Limited 1803–1928* (Grimston: A G M Projects, 1999).

LANE, M. R. (2010), *The story of the Invicta Works: a history of Aveling and Porter, Rochester* (Redditch: National Traction Engine Trust, 2010).

LOCKE, P. G. (1990), 'The Bow McLachlan traction engine', *The Road Locomotive Society Journal*, vol. 43, no. 2, May 1990.

McDONALD, J. (1880), 'On the agriculture of the county of Sutherland', *THASS*, 4th series, vol. XII, 1880.

MACDONALD, J. (1908), *Stephens' book of the farm* (3 vols) (Edinburgh: William Blackwood, 1908).

McEWEN, R. (2007), *The life and rhymes of Robert McEwen: a self portrait* (Stirling, 2007).

J. & H. McLAREN, (1910), *Catalogue of traction engines* (Leeds: J. & H. McLaren, 1910).

J. & H. McLAREN, (1914), *Catalogue of traction engines, Royal Gold Medal steam tractors, steam rollers etc.* (Leeds: J. & H. McLaren, 1914).

McTAGGART, T. (1985), *Pioneers of heavy haulage* (Ayr: Alloway Publishing, 1985).

MARSDEN, B. (2004), *Watt's perfect engine: steam and the age of invention* (Royston: Icon Books, 2004).

MARSHALL, SONS & COMPANY LIMITED (1907), *1907 Catalogue of portable engines, traction engines, thrashing machines, straw elevators, straw trussers, etc.*, publication no. 393, (Gainsborough: Marshall, Sons & Company Limited, 1907)

MARSHALL, SONS & COMPANY LIMITED (1918), *Agricultural engines and machinery*, publication no. 1048 (Gainsborough: Marshall, Sons & Company Limited, 1918).

NASMYTH, J. (S. Smiles, ed.) (1883), *James Nasmyth Engineer: an autobiography* (London: John Murray, 1883).

NATIONAL MUSEUMS OF SCOTLAND (1998), *The Scottish Life Archive [index and guide]* (Edinburgh: National Museums of Scotland, 1998).

THE NATIONAL TRACTION ENGINE OWNERS AND USERS ASSOCIATION (1920), Report of a general meeting, London, 19 May 1920.

OLIVER, G. (1993), *Motor trials and tribulations* (Edinburgh: HMSO, 1993).

PEASE, J. (2003), *The history of J and H McLaren of Leeds* (Ashbourne: Landmark Publishing, 2003).

REID, G. (1991), 'The man who flattened the Devil's Elbow', *The Scots Magazine*, September 1991, vol. 135, no. 6.

REID, J. S. (1990), *Mechanical Aberdeen* (Aberdeen: Keith Murray Publishing/JSR, 1990).

RIDEN, P. (1998), *How to trace the history of your car* (Cardiff: Merton Priory Press, 2nd edition 1998).

ALEXANDER SHANKS & SONS, *Illustrated and descriptive catalogue* (undated, c.1876); *revised price list* (September 1878); *catalogue* (undated, c.1880); *order book* (1882).

SPROTT, G. (1978), *The tractor in Scotland* (Edinburgh: Scottish Country Life Museums Trust, 1978).

SPROTT, G. (1995), *Farming* (Edinburgh: National Museums Scotland, 1995).

TEW, D. (1988), *Traction engines and the law* (Birmingham: National Traction Engine Trust, 2nd edition 1988).

THOMAS, A. R. and THOMAS, J. L. (1992), *An album of 'Sentinel' works photographs: No. 1 Standards and Supers* (Worcester: Woodpecker Publications, 1992).

TINDLEY, A. (2009), '"The Iron Duke": land reclamation and public relations in Sutherland, 1868–95', *Historical Research*, May 2009, vol. 82, no. 216.

TRUE, J. B. and JOHNSON, B. (2008), *The traction engine register* (Crawley: Southern Counties Historic Vehicles Preservation Trust, 2008).

TWEEDDALE, MARQUIS OF (1871), 'Report of special committee of the Highland and Agricultural Society of Scotland appointed to inspect and report on the various systems of cultivating land by steam power in East Lothian', *THASS*, 4th series, vol. III, 1871.

TYLER, C. (1977), *Digging by steam* (Watford: Model and Allied Publications, 1977).

TYLER, C. and HAINING, J. (1970), *Ploughing by steam* (Hemel Hempstead: Model and Allied Publications, 1970).

WEIR, R. (2011), 'King o' the road', *Vintage Spirit*, no. 102, January 2011.

WHITEHEAD, R. A. (1975), *A century of steam-rolling* (London: Ian Allan, 1975).

WILLIAMS, J. A. (1858), *Progressive agriculture: a pamphlet on steam cultivation* (London: James Ridgway, 1858).

WOOD, J. L. (1979), 'A Bray's patent engine by Alex Chaplin & Co., of Glasgow', *The Road Locomotive Society Journal*, vol. 32, no. 2, June 1979.

WOOD, J. L. (2000), *Scottish engineering: the machine makers* (Edinburgh: NMS Publishing Limited, 2000).

WEBSITES

Bon Accord Steam Engine Club, Aberdeen:
www.bonaccordsteamclub.co.uk

Motorbase article on Salvesen steam carriage:
www.motorbase.com/manufacturer/by-id/1486487805

Steam Car Club of Great Britain article on Gurney's steam drag:
www.steamcar.net/artgurn.html

Steam Traction article by J. Alexander on the Thomson road steamer in America:
www.steamtraction.com/article/2007-09-01

Index

NOTE: Page numbers in italics denote image captions; company and business names are shown in bold; and main engine types and other key headings in bold and small capitals.

132